Purposeful Play
for Early Childhood
Phonological Awareness

The ants go marching one by one...

Authors

Hallie Kay Yopp and Ruth Helen Yopp

SHELL EDUCATION

Credits

Publishing Credits

Dona Herweck Rice, *Editor-in-Chief*; Lee Aucoin, *Creative Director*; Don Tran, *Print Production Manager*; Timothy J. Bradley, *Illustration Manager*; Conni Medina, M.A. Ed., *Editorial Director*; Sara Johnson, M.A. Ed., *Senior Editor*; Hillary Wolfe, *Editor*; Robin Erickson, *Interior Layout Designer*; Stephanie Reid, *Cover Designer*; Corinne Burton, M.A. Ed., *Publisher*

Shell Education
5301 Oceanus Drive
Huntington Beach, CA 92649-1030
http://www.shelleducation.com
ISBN 978-1-4258-0665-1
©2011 Shell Educational Publishing, Inc.

A Context for Phonological Awareness

Scientists have contributed a great deal to our understanding of literacy development in recent years. We know, for example, that literacy development begins well before the onset of formal schooling. We know that the experiences children have in their first years contribute tremendously to their later success in reading and writing. We know that literacy is a complex, multifaceted ability that involves much more than recognizing letters and sounding out words. Literacy entails understanding how the written system works, making sense of text content, and making connections among ideas. It requires readers to bring their background knowledge, language, critical-thinking skills, motivation, interests, and experiences to the text.

This book addresses one essential foundation of literacy development: phonological awareness. It provides a definition of phonological awareness, explains why it is important, and describes how it develops. It highlights the crucial role of adults in fostering young children's phonological awareness, and it provides 70 instructional activities that purposefully and explicitly address phonological awareness development while capitalizing on children's joy in play.

Compelling and converging research demands that those who work with young children attend to phonological awareness development. As important as phonological awareness is, however, by itself it means little. Educators must understand the big picture of literacy development, they must understand how children learn and develop in general, and they must know the individual children who populate their classrooms or early childhood settings. Furthermore, they must understand that literacy development is influenced by a child's physical, social, and emotional well-being and by the nature of the relationships formed in the learning environment.

Our hope is that those who work with young children thoughtfully and intentionally use the activities in this book to develop children's phonological awareness in the context of a comprehensive early literacy program and a positive, nurturing environment.

A Brief Lesson in Phonology

Before we discuss phonological awareness, it is important that we share key information about phonology, the sound system of a language. Specifically, we describe *units* of sound: syllables, onsets and rimes, and phonemes.

Throughout this book, sounds will be noted by placement within slash marks, as in /r/. We signify letter names by placing the letters with quotation marks, as in *"r."* (See page 13 for further explanation.)

Syllables

Syllables are uninterrupted sound units organized around a vowel sound. Every syllable has a vowel sound, and that vowel sound may or may not have a consonant sound before or after it. Syllables are sometimes referred to as the "beats" or "pulses" in a word. The following words, as typically spoken, have one syllable: *run*, *cat*, *friend*, *horse*. Notice that the last two words—*friend* and *horse*—have more than one vowel in the spelling of the words. However, they each have only one vowel sound. The letter combination *"ie"* in *friend* makes a single vowel sound. The letter *"e"* in *horse* is not pronounced. Thus, a syllable might be spelled with more than one vowel but have only one vowel sound.

The chart below lists words with two, three, four, and five syllables. Say the words aloud. Can you hear each of the syllables in the words? Try clapping the beats in each of the words.

Just for fun, here are a couple of six-syllable words: *undeliverable* and *misrepresentation*. And, here are a few seven-syllable words: *autobiographical*, *socioeconomic*, and *telecommunication*. An eight-syllable word? *Ultrarevolutionaries*. Perhaps you can think of words with even more syllables!

Two Syllables	Three Syllables	Four Syllables	Five Syllables
bathroom	banana	carbonation	evaporation
breakfast	character	demonstration	intellectual
carpet	dinosaur	lavatory	metamorphosis
easel	elephant	manicurist	misunderstanding
happy	everyone	military	mythological
kitchen	fantasy	miserable	phonological
kitten	grandfather	misunderstand	photosynthesis
pencil	medicine	motorcycle	representative
table	nursery	preparation	unbelievable
water	outfielder	watermelon	vegetarian

A Brief Lesson in Phonology (cont.)

Onsets and Rimes

Syllables can be divided into smaller ("subsyllabic") sound units. One of these smaller units is the *onset* of the syllable. The onset is any consonant sound or blend that precedes the vowel sound in the syllable. For example, the sound /r/ precedes the vowel sound in the single-syllable word *run*. Thus, it is the onset in the syllable. The sounds /st/ precede the vowel sound in the single-syllable word *stop*. Thus, /st/ is the onset in *stop*. Think about the word *grandpa*. How many syllables are in the word? If you said "two," you are correct. What is the onset in the first syllable of the word? The syllable is /grănd/. The onset is /gr/ because /gr/ precedes the vowel in the syllable. What is the onset in the second syllable? The answer is /p/. Sometimes a syllable does not have an onset. For example, think about the single-syllable word *in*. What precedes the vowel in the syllable? Nothing! Therefore, *in* does not contain an onset.

A second subsyllabic unit is the *rime*. The rime unit in a syllable is the vowel sound and any sounds in the syllable that follow it. What is the rime in *him*? The answer is /ĭm/. What is the rime in *flat*? The answer is /ăt/. What is the rime in the first syllable of *fantasy*? The first syllable is /făn/; the rime in this first syllable is /ăn/.

The rime can be divided into a *nucleus* and a *coda*. The nucleus (sometimes called the *peak*) is the vowel sound. The coda consists of any consonant sounds that follow the nucleus in the syllable. Thus, in the one-syllable word *milk*, the onset is /m/ and the rime is /ĭlk/. The rime can be divided into its nucleus and coda, /ĭ/ and /lk/, respectively. The codas of syllables will not be addressed in this book, as they are not generally part of phonological awareness instruction. Speech and language specialists, however, will be impressed that you know about these units!

Phonemes

Phonemes are the smallest sounds of speech. Think about the word *stretch*. It consists of one syllable. The onset and rime in the syllable are /str/ and /ĕch/, respectively. The individual sounds in the word are /s/, /t/, /r/, /ĕ/, and /ch/. These five sounds are the word's phonemes. Listen carefully as you say the word and you will hear each of the phonemes. Here is another example: The spoken word *snail* consists of the phonemes /s/, /n/, /ā/, and /l/. Notice that there are five letters, but there are only four phonemes in the spoken word. Phonemes are the individual sounds we hear, not the letters we see in the printed word.

Spoken English consists of about 43 phonemes (see the chart on page 13). We say "about" because the number depends on the dialect of English spoken and the classification system used. These approximately 43 phonemes make up the entire body of the English language. Imagine that! The hundreds of thousands of words that English speakers use are constructed from only 43 phonemes! (Only 26 letters are used, singly or in combination, to represent these sounds in printed English. The sound /sh/, for example, is represented with two letters: "*sh.*")

A Brief Lesson in Phonology (cont.)

Phonemes (cont.)

Some languages have many more phonemes than English; some have fewer. Spoken Spanish, for example, uses about half the number of sounds that spoken English uses. Typically-developing human beings are physiologically capable of making many sounds with their vocal structures. The phonemes an individual ultimately uses depends upon those heard in the environment. Thus, a child raised in an English-speaking environment hears and will use the phonemes of English. A child raised in a Vietnamese-speaking environment hears and will use the Vietnamese sounds and phonemes.

Some words have only one phoneme. Think about the words I, *a*, and *oh*. Other words, such as *up* and *she*, have two phonemes. Some, such as *dog*, *sick*, and *fun*, have three phonemes. Others have more. The word *sticky* has five phonemes: /s/, /t/, /ĭ/, /k/, /ē/.

Sound Units: A Summary

Sound units of spoken language—from largest to smallest—include syllables, onsets and rimes, and phonemes. The chart below provides the definition and examples of each of these units, followed by charts displaying words divided into these units.

Definitions and Examples of Phonological Units

Speech Unit	Definition	Examples
syllable	A unit of speech consisting of one uninterrupted vowel sound which may or may not be flanked by one or more consonants; uttered with a single impulse of the voice.	man (/măn/) going (/gō/—/ing/) happiness (/hăp/—/ē/—/nĭs/) generation (/jĕn/—/ə/—/rā/—/shən/)
onset	The part of a syllable (consonant or blend) that precedes the vowel. Some syllables do not have an onset.	black (/bl/) go (/g/) friendship (/fr/, /sh/)
rime	The part of a syllable that includes the vowel and any consonants that follow. All syllables have a rime because all syllables have a vowel sound.	run (/ŭn/) catch (/ăch/) in (/ĭn/) captain (/āp/, /ən/)
phoneme	The smallest unit of sound in speech.	/m/, /s/, /t/, /v/, /p/ stop (/s/, /t/, /ŏ/, /p/) ship (/sh/, /ĭ/, /p/)

A Brief Lesson in Phonology (cont.)

Phonological Units in the Word *jump*

Word	jump			
Syllables	jump			
Onsets and Rimes	/j/ (onset)		/ŭmp/ (rime)	
Phonemes	/j/	/ŭ/	/m/	/p/

Phonological Units in the Word *on*

Word	on	
Syllables	on	
Onsets and Rimes	* (onset)	/ŏn/ (rime)
Phonemes		/ŏ/	/n/

* There is no onset in *"on."*

Phonological Units in the Word *chimpanzee*

Word	chimpanzee					
Syllables	/chĭm/		/păn/		/zē/	
Onsets and Rimes	/ch/ (onset)	/ĭm/ (rime)	/p/ (onset)	/ăn/ (rime)	/z/ (onset	/ē/ (rime)
Phonemes	/ch/	/ĭ/	/m/	/p/	/ă/	/n/	/z/	/ē/

Phonological Awareness: A Definition

Phonological awareness (or "phonological sensitivity") is the ability to attend to and manipulate the sounds of spoken language (Burgess 2006; Gillon 2004; Yopp 1992).

A key phrase in this definition is "spoken language." Phonological awareness is about what we hear, not what we see in print.

Another key phrase in this definition is "sounds." Phonological awareness is about reflecting on the sounds of language, not the meaning of language. In fact, phonological awareness demands that children temporarily shift their attention away from the meaning of spoken utterances, to the sounds in those utterances. Individuals who notice sound units in the speech stream (that is, are aware of the phonological structure of spoken language) are demonstrating phonological awareness.

What do we mean by "sounds"? We mean syllables, onsets and rimes, and phonemes—and you know what those are! Phonological awareness encompasses an awareness of any size sound unit. A child who notices and can manipulate the syllable units in speech is said to be phonologically aware at the syllable level. Sometimes we call this *syllable awareness*. Similarly, a child who is able to detect and manipulate the onset and rime units of spoken language is said to be phonologically aware at the onset and rime level. We call this *onset-rime awareness*. A child who can attend to and manipulate the smallest units of sounds, the phonemes, is demonstrating *phoneme* (or *phonemic*) *awareness*—generally the most advanced and

difficult level of phonological awareness (Anthony, Lonigan, Driscoll, Phillips, and Burgess 2003; Lonigan 2006; Phillips, Clancy-Menchetti, and Lonigan 2008; Shaywitz 2003).

Notice that the definition of phonological awareness states it is the ability to attend to (that is, detect, notice, think about, reflect on) and manipulate the sounds of spoken language. What does it mean to "manipulate" the sounds of spoken language? It means to act on the sound units in some way (Adams 1990; Yopp 1988), and, in fact, this is how we know someone is aware of sound units in speech. For example, children may compare or match sounds, as when they determine whether two spoken words begin with the same phoneme. They may synthesize sounds, as when they blend sound units together to form a word. They may analyze sound units, as when they segment a word into its constituent syllables or phonemes, count sound units in a word, or delete sound units from a word. Some manipulations involve both analysis and synthesis of sound units. For example, substitution of sounds requires analysis—segmenting a word into sound units, deleting one sound unit—and synthesis—blending a new sound unit with the remaining sound units. In general, research suggests that analysis tasks are more difficult than synthesis tasks (Phillips et al. 2008; Yopp 1988). The charts on the following pages identify the key elements of the definition of phonological awareness and present a variety of tasks.

Phonological Awareness: A Definition (cont.)

Key Points About Phonological Awareness

Phonological awareness is the ability to attend to and manipulate the sounds of spoken language.

- Phonological awareness is about spoken language, not written language.
- Phonological awareness is about the sounds of spoken language, not the meaning of spoken language.
- Phonological awareness encompasses any size unit of sound, including syllables, onsets and rimes, and phonemes.
- Phonological awareness involves the ability to perform a variety of cognitive operations (such as matching, synthesis, and analysis) on sound units.

Sometimes there is confusion about the terms *phonological awareness*, *phoneme awareness*, and *phonics*. These terms are not synonymous and are not used interchangeably. Both phonological awareness and phoneme awareness refer to an insight about the sound structure of spoken language. Phoneme awareness is a subset of phonological awareness; it is one type of phonological awareness. Phonics is a method of teaching reading that draws learners' attention to the relationship between sounds and the letters that represent them.

Terms and Definitions

Term	Definition
phonological awareness	the ability to attend to and manipulate any size unit of sound in spoken language
phoneme awareness	the ability to attend to and manipulate the smallest unit of sound in spoken language, the phoneme
phonics	a method of teaching reading that focuses on the relationship between sounds and the letters that represent them

#50665—Purposeful Play for Early Childhood Phonological Awareness

Phonological Awareness: A Definition (cont.)

Phonological Awareness Tasks

Task	Syllable	Onset-rime	Phoneme
Matching	Do these start the same? *sandwich, sandbag* (*yes*)	Do these start the same? *start, stand* (*yes*)	Do these start the same? *city, sunshine* (*yes—both words start with the /s/ sound*)
Blending	What word would we have if we put these parts together? /pŭmp/—/kǐn/ (*pumpkin*)	What word would we have if we put these parts together? /pl/—/āne/ (*plane*)	What word would we have if we put these parts (or sounds) together? /f/—/r/—/ŏ/—/g/ (*frog*)
Isolating/ Identifying (partial segmentation)	What do you hear at the beginning of *under*? (/ŭn/)	What do you hear at the beginning of *black*? (/bl/)	What do you hear at the beginning of *bug*? (/b/)
Segmentation	What are the parts (beats or syllables) you hear in this word: *table*? (/tā/—/bəl/)	What are the parts you hear in this word: *spoon*? (/sp/—/ōon/)	What are all the sounds you hear in this word: *dog*? (/d/—/ŏ/—/g/)
Deletion	Say *napkin* without the /kǐn/. (*nap*)	Say *grin* without the /gr/. (*in*)	Say *meat* without the /m/. (*eat*)
Substitution	What word would we have if we changed the /bā/ in *baby* to /mā/? (*maybe*)	What word would we have if we changed the /bl/ in *black* to /cr/? (*crack*)	What word would we have if we changed the /ch/ in *chain* to /r/? (*rain*)

#50665—Purposeful Play for Early Childhood Phonological Awareness

English Speech Sounds

In this book, we will be using the following symbols to represent English phonemes:

Symbol	Sound	Symbol	Sound
/ā/	angel, rain	/g/	gift, dog
/ă/	cat, apple	/h/	happy, hat
/ē/	eat, seed	/j/	jump, bridge
/ĕ/	echo, red	/l/	lip, fall
/ī/	island, light	/m/	mother, home
/ĭ/	in, sit	/n/	nose, on
/ō/	oatmeal, bone	/p/	pencil, pop
/ŏ/	octopus, mom	/r/	rain, care
/ŭ/	up, hum	/s/	soup, face
/ōō/	oodles, moon	/t/	time, cat
/ŏŏ/	put, book	/v/	vine, of
/ə/	above, sofa	/wh/	what, why
/oi/, /oy/	oil, boy	/w/	wet, wind
/ou/, /ow/	out, cow	/y/	yes, beyond
/aw/, /ô/	awful, caught	/z/	zoo, because
/är/	car, far	/th/	thing, health
/ôr/	four, or	/<u>th</u>/	this, brother
/ûr/	her, bird, turn	/sh/	shout, machine
/b/	baby, crib	/zh/	pleasure, vision
/k/	cup, stick	/ch/	children, scratch
/d/	dog, end	/ng/	ring, finger
/f/	phone, golf		

The Importance of Phonological Awareness

Research has consistently shown a strong, immediate, and long-term relationship between phonological awareness and reading achievement, even when accounting for intelligence and socioeconomic status (Ehri, Nunes, Willows, Schuster, Yaghoub-Zadeh, and Shanahan 2001; Gillon 2004; Mann and Foy 2003; National Early Literacy Panel 2008; National Reading Panel 2000). Phonological awareness is one of the strongest predictors of reading success. Without this insight, children are likely to struggle with learning to read.

Why is phonological awareness so important? In many languages, the written system is largely a record of the sounds of the language, specifically the phonemes. For example, in English we represent the spoken word *man* in writing by using symbols that represent the phonemes in the word. The letters *m*, *a*, and *n* represent the sounds /m/, /ă/, /n/. In order to appreciate the logic of the written system, prospective readers must notice that their spoken language consists of sounds. They must become phonologically, even phonemically, aware.

The powerful role of phonological awareness in literacy development becomes obvious when examining the initial writing attempts of young children (Yopp 1999). Children who notice and can mentally capture the sounds in their speech stream (and who understand that we can write what we say and have knowledge of the alphabet) are able to record their ideas in print. A child who writes *sces* for "skis" has noticed the phonemes in speech and uses symbols

(although not the conventional ones) to record those sounds in print. Children who lack this awareness—those who are not yet aware that speech consists of a sequence of sounds—have difficulty writing words other than those they can copy or have memorized. Wanting to write about skis, they might ask an adult how to write the word, find the word in a book, or draw a picture to represent the word. Although these are reasonable approaches, we want to help children become independent users of the written language system.

Phonological awareness is a powerful contributor to literacy development. It enables children to grasp the alphabetic principle and supports their decoding, spelling, and indirectly, comprehension. One of the goals of early literacy programs is to foster phonological awareness (including, eventually, the most advanced level, phoneme awareness). Early childhood educators are in the special position of having the opportunity—and responsibility—to lay this important foundation for success.

Phonological Awareness Development

Research offers some important understandings about how phonological awareness progresses, why it may be difficult to acquire, and what adults can do to promote its development in children.

Progression

Studies reveal that, in general, phonological awareness develops along a continuum, with children's sensitivity to sounds progressing from larger units to smaller units. In other words, children typically first develop an awareness of syllables, then onsets and rimes, and finally phonemes (Anthony et al. 2003; Lonigan 2006; Phillips et al. 2008; Shaywitz 2003).

There is also evidence that some types of manipulations are more challenging than others. In general, children are able to engage in synthesis, or blending, of sounds more readily than they are able to engage in analysis of sounds (Yopp 1988). It is typically easier for children to put the sounds /c/, /ă/, /t/ together to say the word *cat* than it is for them to segment the spoken word *cat* into its individual sounds.

We also know that the position of a sound in a word is related to the difficulty of a phonological awareness activity (Smith, Simmons, and Kame'enui 1998). Children are more likely able to identify the sound at the beginning of a word before they can identify the sound at the end or in the middle of a word. For example, children typically more readily note that /s/ is at the beginning of the word *soap* than that /s/ is at the end of the word *mouse*. Furthermore, phonemes that are a part of a blend are more difficult to notice or manipulate than those not in a blend. Children usually are able to isolate the first sound in *sun*, *hat*, and *fog* earlier than they can isolate the first sound (phoneme, that is—not onset) in *flat*, *trip*, and *black*.

Some researchers suggest that continuant sounds—those that can be stretched—are easier to attend to and manipulate than noncontinuant sounds (Smith, Simmons, and Kame'enui 1998; Yopp 1992). Think about the words *spinach* and *peach*. The /s/ sound at the beginning of the word *spinach* can be elongated, drawing more attention to the sound (*sssssssssspinach*), but the sound at the beginning of *peach* cannot be stretched without a great deal of distortion. *Spinach* begins with a continuant sound (/s/) and *peach* does not (/p/). You can identify continuant sounds by trying to stretch them yourself. Can you sustain the sound? Compare these several continuants, /m/, /f/, /r/, /n/, /l/, /v/, /z/, with these sounds, /t/, /b/, /d/, /k/, /q/.

Finally, children often find it easier to participate in recognition than production tasks (Phillips et al. 2008). For example, children generally can respond to the question, "Does *lamb* begin with /l/?" before they can respond to the question "What sound does *lamb* begin with?"

The chart on the next page summarizes these generalities about the development of phonological awareness. It is important to note that there is no evidence that instruction must take place in a lockstep fashion. Children do not need to master one type of manipulation (such as blending) before they are provided experiences with another (such as segmenting).

Phonological Awareness Development (cont.)

Likewise, they do not need to master manipulations of one size of sound unit (such as syllables) before being offered experiences with another (such as onsets and rimes or phonemes). Nevertheless, an understanding of the general progression can help us design experiences and can be very useful as we work with individuals who find the experiences particularly challenging.

As we consider engaging children in phonological awareness activities, it is also important to recognize the role of adult support. Those who work with young children should be gentle guides, modeling and encouraging children's participation. Adults can also provide support by using pictures and objects. These will help to reduce the memory load required of some activities. For example, a child may be shown two pictures, perhaps one of a flower and one of a tree, when considering which spoken word—*flower* or *tree*—begins with the onset /fl/. Likewise, a child can handle several familiar objects (such as a sock, clock, and paintbrush), name them, and then determine which two have the same rime unit. Having pictures or objects available lessens the challenge of the task. Similarly, adults can have children use blocks or chips to represent sound units, thus making the units more concrete. Eventually, letters should replace the objects.

General Development of Phonological Awareness

Think about moving from…

> larger units ➡ smaller units
>
> matching and synthesis ➡ analysis
>
> initial sounds ➡ final and medial (middle) sounds
>
> phonemes that are not in blends ➡ those that are in blends
>
> continuant sounds ➡ noncontinuant sounds
>
> recognition ➡ production
>
> use of pictures and objects ➡ oral-only activities
>
> use of objects such as chips or blocks (to represent sounds) ➡ use of letters

Phonological Awareness Development (cont.)

The Difficulty with Phonological Awareness

Phonological awareness can be difficult for children. Although it may seem obvious to us that speech is made up of sounds, it is not obvious to young children. Phonological awareness requires that children temporarily turn their attention away from the meaning of speech (the message that is being conveyed) to the sounds of speech. Phonological awareness activities require children to think about the sound structure of speech rather than what a spoken utterance means (Ehri and Roberts 2006; Yopp 1992).

Phoneme awareness is particularly difficult because phonemes are co-articulated: That is, they overlap one another in speech (Liberman, Shankweiler, Fischer, and Carter 1974; Valtin 1984; Yopp 1992). In fact, how a phoneme is formed by the mouth is influenced by the sounds that precede or follow it. Say the word *dig* aloud. Say it again and concentrate on what your mouth is doing as you begin the word. What are your lips and tongue doing? Now say the word *do* aloud. Say it again and notice what your lips and tongue are doing. Now say both words again and stop just before each word is spoken. Do you notice a difference between the way your mouth prepares for *dig* and the way it prepares for *do*? Although the two words begin with the same phoneme, /d/, your mouth is positioned differently because of the sounds that follow /d/. Thinking about phonemes as individual units can be difficult, especially when they are influenced by the sounds that surround them!

In spite of these potential difficulties, most children can become phonologically—even phonemically—aware.

Fostering Phonological Awareness

How do children become phonologically aware? Studies have demonstrated that most children who engage in activities that explicitly focus their attention on sound units develop phonological awareness (National Early Literacy Panel 2008; National Reading Panel 2000). Early childhood settings should be phonologically rich, offering children many opportunities to notice and manipulate sounds. Some of those opportunities will be spontaneous, as when an adult notices a child playing with sounds and capitalizes on the moment (Yopp and Yopp 2009). For example, if a child is chanting "mamama, hahaha, lalala," the adult might comment on the fun and add to it: "Listen to you change sounds! I can do that, too. I'll start with /w/: Wawawa! Let's try another sound!"

Other opportunities will be deliberately planned and will involve explicit instruction and guidance. Instruction may include the use of children's books, songs, and games that focus on sound manipulation, and other activities that prompt exploration of and reflection on sounds (Yopp 1992, 1995; Yopp and Yopp 2000, 2002, 2009). The adult will prepare an activity, engage small groups of children, offer clear explanations and provide examples, observe and guide children's responses, provide feedback, then thoughtfully design follow-up experiences.

Phonological Awareness Development (cont.)

Fostering Phonological Awareness (cont.)

Each of these approaches—spontaneous and planned—is important and has a place in the early childhood setting. Each approach should be guided by the adult's knowledge of phonological awareness, the children, and appropriate practices with young children in general.

It is important to note that, in addition to experiences with sound units, two other factors appear to contribute to the development of phonological awareness (Burgess 2006; Lonigan 2006). One of these is letter knowledge. Some studies suggest that the acquisition of letter knowledge (associating a sound with a letter more than knowing the letter name) is related to the development of phonological awareness. Phonological awareness, in turn, facilitates letter knowledge.

The other factor is oral language. The larger a child's vocabulary, the more likely it is that he or she will develop phonological awareness. As children learn more and more words that share sounds, they must attend more closely to the smaller parts of the words. Notice that you don't have to pay much attention to the parts of the spoken words *rhinoceros* and *happy* to distinguish between them; however, you do need to attend more closely to the individual sounds (particularly the final sound) in *cup* and *cut* to distinguish between these two spoken words. As "neighborhood density" (the number of words sharing sounds)

increases, it is likely that the demand for attention to the smaller sounds in those words increases (Lonigan 2006).

These findings suggest that environments that support children's letter knowledge and that offer many rich language experiences to build their vocabulary have the added benefit of contributing to phonological awareness development. However, they do not replace thoughtful and explicit attention to phonological awareness.

Supporting English Language Learners' Development of Phonological Awareness

Evidence suggests that, like many skills and abilities, phonological awareness transfers from one language to another (Yopp and Stapleton 2008). A child who has developed phonological awareness in his or her native language brings that insight to a second language. (However, the child will still have new sounds to learn.) Thus, it is advantageous for children to become phonologically aware in their native language. Some ways to support phonological awareness in the native language are listed on the following page. Similarly, sensitive attention must be given to supporting phonological awareness in the second language. General guidelines for fostering phonological awareness in English are also provided on the following page.

Phonological Awareness Development (cont.)

Fostering Phonological Awareness for the English Language Learner

To support phonological awareness development in the native language, consider the following:

- Identify songs, books, rhymes, chants, and games that play with sounds in the native language. Teach them to children, emphasizing the sound play, as suggested in many of the activities in this book.

- Enlist the support of parents. Share activities with them. Draw upon their knowledge of playful sound manipulation activities.

- Carefully select activities from this book that are suitable for translation. However, keep in mind that simple translations are rarely appropriate. For example, a one-syllable word in English may not have a one-syllable translation or may not begin with the targeted sound. Think about the intention and spirit of each activity and develop a parallel activity in the native language, if possible.

To support phonological awareness development in English, consider the following:

- Draw upon English words that are familiar to the children, such as their names or familiar classroom items. Begin with what children know.

- Repeat the activities frequently as repetition is helpful to those new to a language.

- Value children's native language responses. For example, if you show a picture of a cat as part of a rhyming activity and a child says the word for cat in his or her native language, affirm the response before sharing the English word and continuing the activity.

- Be especially thoughtful about how activities are introduced and shared. Be explicit with directions, model the activities, guide children, and provide clear feedback.

- Learn about the child's native language. Sounds that exist in English but do not exist in the native language will need particular attention. For example, the /ă/ sound in *man* does not exist in Spanish and /st/ does not occur at the beginning of words. Be sensitive to phonology differences among languages. Capitalize on similarities.

- Pronounce sounds clearly, particularly those that are not a part of the native language.

- Provide support, share as many examples as needed, and make use of visuals (such as objects and picture cards).

- Be positive and encouraging. Establish a psychologically safe environment so children feel comfortable taking risks.

A Word About Word Awareness

Some researchers and educators include word awareness in their discussions of phonological awareness (Lonigan 2006; Phillips et al. 2008). Word awareness is the ability to attend to and manipulate individual words in spoken sentences, phrases, or compounds. For example, a child with word awareness knows that the sentence, I *have a friendly dog*, consists of individual words. The child can segment the phrase *the purple cow* into its three words—*the, purple,* and *cow*—and can substitute one word with another, changing *purple* to *brown: the brown cow.* The child knows that deleting the second word from the compound word *firefighter* results in the word *fire.* Words are units of language, and the same types of manipulations that can be done with syllables, onsets and rimes, and phonemes (see page 12) can be done with words.

However, word awareness is not a phonological understanding (Moats and Tolman 2008). Words are meaning-based, not sound-based, units of language. Nouns (*car, telephone*), adjectives (*blue, new*), verbs (*jump, run*), and adverbs (*slowly, yesterday*) obviously convey meaning; function words (*the, an*) convey meaning in a less obvious way. Phonological awareness is, as we noted throughout this chapter, an awareness of the sound structure of language.

Nevertheless, word awareness is an important skill to foster. It helps children understand how print is laid out on a page—children begin to understand what the spaces surrounding groups of symbols signify. More relevant to our discussion, however, is the fact that, like phonological awareness, word awareness is a metalinguistic skill; that is, it demands that children think about language itself. Language, then, becomes more than the medium by which we communicate with one another: it becomes an object of attention. This same type of shift of attention is required for phonological awareness.

Assessment

Phonological awareness is an important foundation upon which many later literacy insights are constructed. Children in early childhood settings have the right to be with adults who attend to the development of their phonological awareness. This means more than providing phonological awareness instruction; it includes monitoring children's progress so that meaningful and appropriate experiences can be offered. Although there will be occasions when adults formally assess children's phonological awareness development, much can be learned about children's progress through daily observations and interactions.

Each of the activities in this book presents an opportunity for an adult to learn about a child's phonological awareness development. Effective teachers provide instruction; they model and engage children in learning experiences; they notice and reflect on children's responses; they provide feedback, and then plan future instruction based on what they have learned about the children. Some children will quickly embrace an activity and demonstrate understanding of the phonological manipulations. When a teacher uses a puppet to encourage children to change initial sounds in peers' names to the /m/ sound, and a child responds, "Billy is Milly! Danny is Manny!", the teacher notices this and later records it in the anecdotal journal he or she keeps. Other children will find an activity more challenging. If a child does not understand the phonological play in an activity, the teacher may decide to provide more explicit instruction and practice or to provide more scaffolding. Depending upon the response to modified instruction, the teacher may decide to build more of a foundation before trying the activity again

at a later time. A review of the General Development of Phonological Awareness chart on page 16 will be helpful.

The information teachers gather as they observe children during directed and independent activities, and teachers' willingness to engage in reflection before, during, and after an instructional activity, contribute greatly to effective teaching that meets the needs of the children. The questions on the following pages focus on progress monitoring and guide reflection.

Note: All formal assessments must be used with care. Adults must ensure the assessments are valid; used for appropriate purposes such as planning meaningful learning experiences; are linguistically, culturally, and developmentally appropriate; and are not the sole basis of important decisions impacting children's lives. Furthermore, adults conducting the assessments must be adequately prepared to implement and interpret them. A discussion of formal assessment is beyond the scope of this book.

Assessment

Before the Activity

Questions	Things to Consider
• Why am I choosing this activity for this group of children?	• Who are the children? • What is their current understanding? How do I know? • Is the activity challenging, yet achievable, for these children? • What is the purpose of the activity? • How does the activity fit in the bigger picture of phonological awareness development?
• How should I implement the activity? • How might I modify the activity?	• Shall I use the activity with individuals? small groups? the entire group? • Do I need to modify the activity to be appropriate for certain children?
• What will serve as evidence of understanding?	• What will I look for to determine whether the activity is appropriate and whether children understand it? • Will I watch to see if children generate a rhyming word? blend an onset and rime together to form a word? delete a phoneme from the beginning of a word? • Will I notice who is pointing, speaking, or nodding?

Assessment (cont.)

During the Activity

Questions	Things to Consider
• How are children responding as a group—cognitively, socially, and emotionally?	• As a group, do children provide correct responses? • Do they attend to and participate in the activity? • Do they find it appealing? • Do they appear confident, enthusiastic and happy, or are they anxious, restless, frustrated, or bored? • Do they ask to play again?
• How are children responding individually—cognitively, socially, and emotionally?	• Do I ever choose to closely observe an individual during an activity? • Is this child silent, yet attentive? quick to respond? accurate? enthusiastic? • Does he or she go beyond the activity and create other, more sophisticated language play? • Is this child distracted? uncomfortable? • Does he or she give inaccurate responses? • How does this child respond when more explicit explanations and gentle specific feedback are given? • Does this child seek out the materials to play again later?
• Is a small or large group activity of value even to those children who appear to understand it less than their peers?	• Is this activity appropriate for and appealing to even those children who do not appear to fully understand it yet? • Do those children appear to appreciate the activity—even just for its silliness—and learn from their exposure to it? or are they experiencing frustration or feelings of inadequacy? • What is my role in influencing how children feel when faced with more challenging activities?

Assessment (cont.)

After the Activity

Questions	Things to Consider
• What might I have done differently?	• Was I engaging? positive? enthusiastic? respectful of linguistic and cultural differences? • Was I explicit in providing directions? • Did I model? • Did I explain what we were doing and why responses were correct or incorrect? • Did I provide specific feedback? • Did I gently guide children? • How was my pacing? • Did I provide enough time for children to think and respond? • Did I provide too much time for a single child to respond so that others became disengaged and bored? • Did I make anyone uncomfortable? • When I do this activity again, what will I change?
• What should I do next?	• Which children need more individual attention from me? • With whom will I follow up with additional opportunities to engage in this or a similar activity? • What do children now understand? • What are they ready to try or be exposed to next? smaller units of sound? different types of manipulations? the same units of sound and manipulations with other materials or examples? • When will I repeat this activity? • How will I ensure that children have multiple opportunities to engage in similar phonological play? • Will I find ways to spontaneously follow up on this kind of play in other contexts during the day?

Overview of the Activities

In this book, we offer 70 activities that support phonological awareness development. We begin with several activities that address word awareness. These activities prompt children to reflect on language and to begin to think about its parts. Children blend, segment, delete, and substitute words in sentences, phrases, and compound words.

The Word Awareness section is followed by sections that focus on syllables, onsets and rimes, and phonemes, thus progressing from larger units of sound to smaller units of sound. We include matching, synthesis (blending), and analysis (segmentation, counting, deletion, and substitution) activities. Some activities focus on initial sounds, some on final sounds, and some on all sounds. We have ordered our activities within each section in a way that generally reflects what experts suggest about the development of phonological awareness. However, there is no research that indicates we must strictly adhere to an order of presentation. Furthermore, you will find that children may experience more success with the simpler phoneme awareness activities (such as matching initial phonemes) than with more complex syllable activities (such as deleting syllables).

At the start of each section we include a chart that identifies the units and operations that each activity entails. Each activity includes the standard(s) addressed, the purpose (in terms of phonological development), a brief overview, the materials needed, and the procedure to follow, as well as ways to modify or extend the activity for struggling or more advanced children. Because

partnerships with families benefit children greatly, we also include suggestions for home connections for each activity and provide a letter describing phonological awareness that may be given to families (written in both English and Spanish). These are also available on the Teacher Resource CD.

Before sharing the activities, adults may wish to use some of the suggested listening activities below. These activities are intended to encourage children to listen attentively. The ability to listen is crucial for the development of phonological awareness. Thus, these activities lay the groundwork for the careful listening skills required by the phonological awareness activities in this book.

Prepare Learners with Listening Activities

- Tell children you will ask them to close their eyes and listen carefully to the sounds around them. Alert them that they will be asked to say what they heard when their eyes were closed. Model by closing your eyes, listening for a few seconds, and then opening your eyes and telling the children what you heard. Then, ask the children to close their eyes and listen carefully. After a moment, tell them to open their eyes. Encourage the children to share with you and one another the sounds they heard.

- Show two familiar objects to the children. Make a sound with each. For example, you may ring a bell and beat on a drum. Ask the children to watch and listen carefully as you make both sounds. Then, tell them to close their eyes.

Overview of the Activities (cont.)

You make one of the sounds; their job is to identify it. Repeat this several times. Let a child select one of the objects while the other children close their eyes to guess. Play the game again with other objects. You might flip the pages in a book, tap a pencil on the floor, punch the buttons on a cell phone, or pour water from one cup to another. Let the children propose sounds for the game. Invite them to bring objects from home.

- Have children identify a sequence of sounds. Use familiar sound-making objects (such as a bell, timer, and whistle) to make sounds, one after the other. Ask the children to tell you what they hear, in order. After demonstrating and ensuring that the children understand, ask them to close their eyes. Make two sounds, then have the children open their eyes and tell you what they heard, in order. Begin with two sounds, then progress to three and four.

- Play "Follow the Leader" with musical instruments or other objects that make sounds. Provide a selection of identical instruments or sound makers to each child. Make one sound, then a second. Ask the children to repeat the sounds in the same order as they heard them. Begin with two sounds, then progress to three and four. Let a volunteer be the leader after the game is understood.

- Play "Who Is Speaking?" Ask a volunteer to sit the middle of a in a circle of several of his or her peers. Each child in the circle says the sentence, "Aknesa is my friend,"

using the name of the volunteer, who watches and listens carefully. The child in the center then closes his or her eyes. Select a child in the circle to say the sentence. The child in the center then opens his or her eyes and is given several chances to guess the speaker.

- Play the traditional version of "Simon Says." Children must listen carefully for the words "Simon Says" and to the directions "Simon" provides. Begin with one direction, such as "Simon says stand up." Increase the number of directions over time, with two, three, and four directions. An example of two directions is as follows: "Simon says stand up and turn around."

- Share books that emphasize sounds in nature. *We're Going on a Bear Hunt* (Rosen 1997), *The Listening Walk* (Showers 1993), and *Off We Go!* (Yolen 2000) are excellent choices. Talk about the sounds.

- Sing songs, such as "The Hokey Pokey," that require children to follow instructions. Model the motions at first, then later sing it without modeling so children rely on listening rather than watching.

- Play "Telephone." Have children sit in a circle. Think of a three- or four-word sentence (or longer with older children) and whisper it to the child to your right. This child whispers the sentence to the next child. The message is whispered from one child to the next. The last child who hears the message says it aloud. Tell children the original sentence and discuss how the sentence changed as it was passed along.

Tips for Success

Phonological awareness is a crucial foundation of literacy and those who work with young children have a key role in promoting its development. Addressing phonological awareness development should be an enjoyable, positive and purposeful endeavor. As you implement the activities in this book, please keep the following in mind.

1. Be playful.

- Young children embrace and learn much through play. In the early childhood setting, phonological awareness instruction should be playful. As you engage children with the activities in this book, smile and laugh. Capitalize on children's interest in fun. Children are more likely to engage in activities that they find enjoyable.

- Be creative and encourage children's creativity. Use your imagination and prompt children to experiment with sounds in many ways throughout the day.

2. Be explicit.

- Draw children's attention to the sound play and talk about the sounds and the sound manipulations in the activities. Explain and model. Provide plenty of examples and guidance. Do not assume that children will grasp the phonological manipulations in the activities without your direct input.

- Be attentive to children's responses and provide appropriate and specific feedback, affirming or gently correcting children's responses and providing additional explanations, examples, and support as needed.

3. Ensure rich exposure.

- Engage children in the activities more than once. They can be enjoyed repeatedly over the course of weeks.

- Be sensitive to individual differences and consider which activities are most appropriate for which children, but do not assume that children who are quieter are not benefitting from the exposure. Do not demand mastery of one activity before sharing another.

- Recognize that phonological awareness can be fostered throughout the day in a variety of contexts. Continue to play with sounds after the children have enjoyed an activity.

4. Pronounce sounds with care.

- If you are unsure of the pronunciation of a sound, check with a friend or colleague.

- Avoid adding /ŭ/ to the end of sounds. The phoneme /h/, not the syllable /hŭ/, is what we hear at the beginning of *hot*. Think about the confusion that is created when a child is told that the sounds /hŭ/-/ŏ/-/tŭ/ make the word *hot*. Actually, they make the nonsense word *huhotuh*. Use the same care with the pronunciation of any size sound unit. For example, the onset /st/ (as in *stop*) should not be pronounced /stŭ/.

- When stretching a sound (such as /mmmm/), avoid changing the pitch. A sing-song like presentation of a sound can be confusing.

Tips for Success (cont.)

Each section begins with a descriptive overview of the objectives. Then, a chart of all the activities is included to show the target skill for each activity.

Every activity includes the standard(s) addressed, a description of its purpose, and a brief overview.

The Home Connection shows you how to empower families to reinforce these skills.

We provide a sample of the activity materials or we offer suggested sentences or words for each activity to help you prepare.

The materials needed are shown (including whether they are available on the Teacher Resource CD), and a simple step-by-step procedure is provided. In addition, ways to modify or extend the activity to accommodate diverse learners are included.

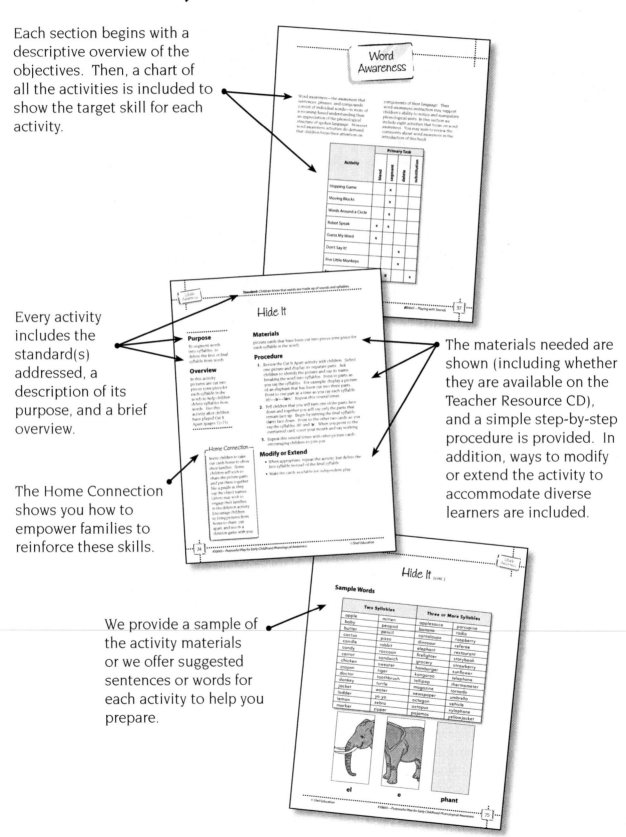

Tips for Success *(cont.)*

Picture Cards

Many of the activities recommend using picture cards. Download pictures from the Internet, find them in magazines or other print sources, or borrow pictures from existing materials in your class. Sample picture cards are included with many activities, and more are available on the Teacher Resource CD.

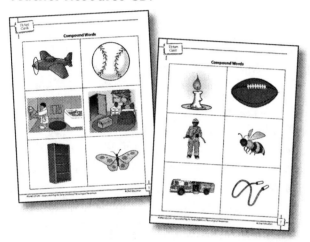

Letter to Families

A sample letter is provided (in English and Spanish) on pages 30–31, and also on the Teacher Resource CD, to show how you can introduce families to the kinds of activities being used in class and to begin building a relationship for a strong home connection.

Children's Literature

Some of the activities in this book rely on children's literature, chants, poems, and songs. We list the books and titles in a bibliography section at the end of the book (pages 188–189). Take time to gather these materials and become familiar with them in advance.

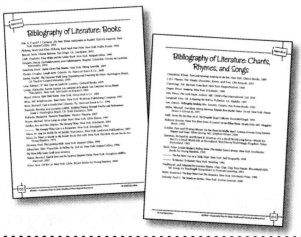

A Letter for Families

Dear Families,

An important way to support your child's reading development is to play with the sounds of language. Research shows that when children are aware that speech consists of small sounds, this positively affects their progress in learning to read. This awareness is called *phonological awareness*. Early childhood educators all over the world are incorporating playful language activities into their programs in order to foster children's phonological awareness. The activities are playful and silly, but they serve an important purpose: They draw children's attention to the sounds of spoken language.

Here are a few things you can do to help heighten your child's awareness of sounds:

- **Read aloud books that draw attention to sounds.** Enjoy the books with your child and comment on the language play. Excellent examples of books that play with sounds include Dr. Seuss's *There's a Wocket in My Pocket!*, Janie Bynum's *Altoona Baboona*, and Anna Dewdney's *Llama, Llama Red Pajama*. Ask your local librarian for others.

- **Sing songs that play with sounds.** Do you know "This Old Man," "A-Hunting We Will Go," "Willoughby Wallaby Woo," or "The Name Game"? Ask your child about the songs we sing together. Notice that some of the songs rhyme, some change the sounds in words, and some break words into syllables or smaller sounds. Children delight in these songs. Enjoy them with your child!

- **Share poems that play with sounds.** Many poetry books include a section on silly poems that rhyme, repeat sounds, or otherwise emphasize sounds. Ask your local librarian for a poetry anthology. Look for poems that use silly or nonsense sounds.

- **Play guessing games that focus on sounds.** While eating together, tell your child you are thinking of something in front of you that sounds like *palt*. (salt) As your child is getting dressed, say you are thinking of something he or she is wearing that begins with the sound /sh/. (*shoes*)

- **Visit us and ask me about other ways we engage in phonological play!**

Phonological awareness is important. Fortunately, there is much fun to be had in sparking its development. Enjoy these experiences with your child!

Sincerely,

A Letter for Families

Queridas familias,

Una manera importante de apoyar el desarrollo de la lectura de su hijo/a es jugar con los sonidos del lenguaje. La investigación muestra que cuando los estudiantes están conscientes de que la habla consiste de sonidos pequeños, esto afecta positivamente su progreso en el aprendizaje de la lectura. Esta conciencia se llama conciencia fonológica. Los educadores de los niños pequeños de todo el mundo están incorporando en sus programas actividades juguetonas basadas en el lenguaje para fomentar la conciencia fonológica. Estas actividades son cómicas y juguetonas, pero sirven un propósito importante: Centran la atención de los estudiantes en los sonidos del idioma hablado.

Aquí están unas cosas que usted puede hacer para ayudar a realzar la conciencia de su hijo/a de los sonidos:

- **Lea libros en voz alta que centren la atención en los sonidos.** Disfruten de los libros con su hijo/a, y comente en el juego del lenguaje. Unos ejemplos excelentes de libros que juegan con los sonidos incluyen *¡Hay un molillo en mi bolsillo!* por Dr. Seuss, *Números tragaldabas* por M. Robleda y *¡Pío Peep!*, Rimas tradicionales en español por A.F. Ada y F.I. Campoy. Pídale más a su bibliotecario local.

- **Canten canciones que jueguen con los sonidos.** ¿Conoce "Una mosca parada en la pared", "Los pollitos" o "La mar estaba serena"? Pregúntele a su hijo/a sobre las canciones que cantamos juntos. Note que algunas de las canciones riman, algunas cambian los sonidos de las palabras, y algunas descomponen las palabras en sílabas o sonidos más pequeños. Los estudiantes gozan de estas canciones. ¡Disfruten de ellas con su hijo/a!

- **Compartan poemas que jueguen con los sonidos.** Muchos libros de poesía incluyen una sección sobre poemas cómicos que riman, repiten sonidos o resaltan los sonidos. Pídale a su bibliotecario local que le ayude a encontrar una antología de poesía. Busque poemas que usen sonidos cómicos o imaginarios.

- **Jueguen a las adivinanzas usando sonidos.** Mientras comen, dígale a su hijo/a que usted está pensando en algo frente a usted que suene como *pal.* (sal) Mientras su hijo/a se viste, dígale que usted está pensando de algo que empiece con el sonido /s/. (*zapatos*)

- **¡Visítenos y pregúnteme sobre las otras formas que nos enfocamos en el juego fonológico!**

La conciencia fonológica es importante. Afortunadamente, hay mucha diversión por experimentar en desarrollarla. ¡Disfruten de estas experiencias con su hijo/a!

Sinceramente,

Correlations to Standards

Shell Education is committed to producing educational materials that are research and standards based. In this effort, we have correlated all of our products to the academic standards of all 50 states, the District of Columbia, and the Department of Defense Dependents Schools.

How to Find Standards Correlations

To print a customized correlation report of this product for your state, visit our website at **http://www.shelleducation.com** and follow the on-screen directions. If you require assistance in printing correlation reports, please contact Customer Service at 1-877-777-3450.

Purpose and Intent of Standards

The No Child Left Behind legislation mandates that all states adopt academic standards that identify the skills children will learn in kindergarten through grade twelve. While many states had already adopted academic standards prior to NCLB, the legislation set requirements to ensure the standards were detailed and comprehensive.

Standards are designed to focus instruction and guide adoption of curricula. Standards are statements that describe the criteria necessary for children to meet specific academic goals. They define the knowledge, skills, and content children should acquire at each level. Standards are also used to develop standardized tests to evaluate children's academic progress.

Teachers are required to demonstrate how their lessons meet state standards. State standards are used in development of all of our products, so educators can be assured they meet the academic requirements of each state.

McREL Compendium

We use the Mid-continent Research for Education and Learning (McREL) Compendium to create standards correlations. Each year, McREL analyzes state standards and revises the compendium. By following this procedure, McREL is able to produce a general compilation of national standards. Each lesson in this product is based on one or more McREL standards. The charts on the following pages list each standard taught in this product and the page numbers for the corresponding lessons.

TESOL Standards

The lessons in this book promote English language development for English language learners. The standards listed on the following pages support the language objectives presented throughout the lessons.

Correlations to Standards (cont.)

Activity	Standard			
	Children discriminate among the sounds of spoken language.	Children know that words are made up of sounds and syllables.	Children know rhyming sounds and simple rhymes.	Children use basic elements of phonetic word analysis.
Hopping Game, p. 38	X			
Moving Blocks, p. 40	X			
Word Around a Circle, p. 42	X			
Robot Speak, p. 44	X			
Guess My Word, p. 46	X			
Don't Say It!, p. 48	X			
Five Little Monkeys, p. 50		X		
Sentence Strips, p. 52		X		
Have You Ever Heard Some Children?, p. 56		X		
Clap, Clap, Clap Your Hands, p. 58		X		
Bearsie Bear, p. 60		X		
Dracula, p. 62		X		
Count the Syllables, p. 64		X		
Copycat, p. 66		X		
Sort the Cards, p. 68		X		
Syllable Turn Taking, p. 70		X		
Cut It Apart, p. 72		X		
Hide It, p. 74		X		
There Was a Teacher, p. 76		X		
Reverse!, p. 78	X			
The Hungry Thing, p. 82		X	X	
The Hungry Thing Goes to a Restaurant, p. 84		X	X	
Rhymes in a Bag, p. 86		X	X	
Add a Verse, p. 88		X	X	
A Tisket, A Tasket, p. 90		X	X	
Hickory Dickory Dock, p. 92		X	X	
To Market! To Market!, p. 94		X	X	
Jamberry, p. 96		X	X	
Web of Words, p. 98		X	X	
The Ants Go Marching, p. 100		X	X	
I Spy, p. 102		X	X	
The Mystery Bag, p. 104		X	X	
Ring Around the Rosy, p. 106		X	X	
Mail a Package, p. 108		X	X	
Going on a Word Hunt, p. 110		X	X	

Correlations to Standards *(cont.)*

Activity	Children discriminate among the sounds of spoken language.	Children know that words are made up of sounds and syllables.	Children know rhyming sounds and simple rhymes.	Children use basic elements of phonetic word analysis.
I Say, You Say, p. 112		X	X	
Trip! Trap!, p. 114		X	X	
Puppet Play, p. 116		X	X	
Sound Snacks, p. 120	X	X		
What Is My Word?, p. 122	X	X		
Do You Know?, p. 124	X	X		
Concentration, p. 126	X	X		
Willoughby Wallaby, p. 128	X	X		
Cock-a-Doodle-Moo!, p. 130	X	X		
Sound Bingo, p. 132	X	X		
Pop! Goes the Weasel, p. 134	X	X		
The Farmer in the Dell, p. 136	X	X		
Head, Shoulders, Knees, and Toes, p. 138	X	X		
Bappy Birthday Boo Boo, p. 140	X	X		
Find Your Partner, p. 142	X	X		
The Golden Touch, p. 144	X	X		
Odd One Out!, p. 146	X	X		
The Line Game, p. 148	X	X		
Can You Help Me with These Sounds?, p. 150	X	X		
If You Think You Know This Word, p. 152	X	X		
Turn It Over!, p. 154	X	X		
Segmenting Sam, p. 156	X	X		
Slow Motion Speech, p. 158	X	X		
Beginning, Middle, or End?, p. 160	X	X		
Elkonin Sound Boxes, p. 162	X	X		
Break It!, p. 164	X	X		
Simon Says, p. 166	X	X		
Post That Letter!, p. 170	X			X
Sound Sort, p. 172	X	X		X
Make a Change, p. 174	X	X		X
Willoughby Wallaby with Letters, p. 176	X	X		X
"A" Was Once an Apple Pie, p. 178	X	X		X
Draw a Card, p. 180	X	X		X
Add a Sound, p. 182	X	X		X
Make a Word, p. 184	X	X		X

#50665—Purposeful Play for Early Childhood Phonological Awareness © Shell Education

TESOL Standards Chart

TESOL Standard	Activity
Students will use English to participate in social interactions	All activities
Students will interact in, through, and with spoken and written English for personal expression and enjoyment	All activities
Students will use learning strategies to extend their communicative competence	All activities
Students will use English to interact in the classroom	All activities
Students will use English to obtain, process, construct, and provide subject matter information in spoken and written form	All activities
Students will use appropriate learning strategies to construct and apply academic knowledge	All activities
Students will use the appropriate language variety, register, and genre according to audience, purpose, and setting	All activities
Students will use nonverbal communication appropriate to audience, purpose, and setting	All activities
Students will use appropriate learning strategies to extend their sociolinguistic and sociocultural competence	All activities

#50665—Purposeful Play for Early Childhood Phonological Awareness

Word Awareness

Word awareness—the awareness that sentences, phrases, and compounds consist of individual words—is more of a meaning-based understanding than an appreciation of the phonological structure of spoken language. However, word awareness activities do demand that children focus their attention on components of their language. Thus, word awareness instruction may support children's ability to notice and manipulate phonological units. In this section we include eight activities that focus on word awareness. You may wish to review the comments about word awareness in the introduction of this book.

Activity	Primary Task			
	blend	segment	delete	substitute
Hopping Game		x		
Moving Blocks		x		
Words Around a Circle		x		
Robot Speak	x	x		
Guess My Word	x	x		
Don't Say It!			x	
Five Little Monkeys			x	
Sentence Strips		x		x

Standard: Children discriminate among the sounds of spoken language.

Hopping Game

Purpose

To segment sentences into words

Overview

The teacher shares a short sentence. Children hop or step from one colored mat to another as they repeat each word in the sentence. This activity should be implemented with very small groups of children so movement is easy and the teacher can observe whether children are hopping as each word is said.

Materials

small mats on which individual children may stand (or squares marked with masking tape on the floor, or chalk squares drawn on concrete or blacktop outdoors)

Procedure

1. Place mats or draw squares next to each other on the floor, close enough for children to easily hop or step from one to another. There should be more squares than there are children in the group and at least as many as there are words in the sentences you use.

2. Ask each child to stand on a mat or square. Say a short sentence, and ask children to repeat it. (Sample sentences are presented on the next page.)

3. Say the sentence again. This time when children repeat the sentence, they hop to a different mat or square for each word they say—one mat or square per word.

Modify or Extend

- Start with sentences that have single-syllable words. Gradually, use sentences that have words with more than one syllable. Add to the fun by including the children's names in the sentences.

- Allow children to generate their own sentences if they like. Repeat the sentences and hop!

┌─ Home Connection ─┐

Send home chalk or masking tape so children can play the game with their families. If you have a class or center web page, consider posting the instructions for this activity, along with sample sentences.

Hopping Game (cont.)

Sample Sentences

One-syllable Words	Multisyllabic Words
She jumps.	I like tacos.
The dog ran.	Jamal ran upstairs.
She ate corn.	The teacher is happy.
He climbs a tree.	Children are playful.
The cat is black.	Rabbits and kangaroos are cute.
He saw a snake.	Sherry ate pancakes for breakfast.
The sky is blue.	Please eat your carrots.
Wash your hands.	I enjoy walking my dog.
She has long hair.	Bananas are delicious!

© Shell Education   #50665—Purposeful Play for Early Childhood Phonological Awareness

Standard: Children discriminate among the sounds of spoken language.

Moving Blocks

Purpose

To segment sentences into words

Overview

The teacher shows children how to move blocks, chips, or other items for each word they hear in a sentence.

Materials

blocks, chips, or other small items

Procedure

1. Provide each child with at least as many small blocks or chips as there are words in the longest sentence you share. Have children place their items in piles in front of them.

2. As you say a sentence, children move one block or chip from their piles for each word. Model the activity by sharing several sentences. Sample sentences are shown on the next page.

3. Ask children to listen to a sentence. First, say it naturally. Then repeat it slowly, pausing between each word. As children repeat the sentence with you, they move their blocks or chips for each word. Provide support as needed.

4. Ask children to create their own sentences. The class repeats them and moves blocks for each word.

Modify or Extend

- Start with simple two- or three-word sentences with single-syllable words. Later, add multisyllabic words.

- Have each child in a circle contribute a block for a different word. For example, Daniel places a block in the middle of the circle for the first word in the sentence, then Juan places a block in the circle for the second word, and so forth.

─Home Connection─

Tell children that they do not have to use blocks to play this game. They can move stuffed animals or shoes or other objects they have at home for each word in a sentence. Encourage them to play at home with their families or invite them to bring in objects to share with the group.

Moving Blocks (cont.)

Sample Sentences

One-syllable Words	Multisyllabic Words
She sings.	I like pizza.
The cat hid.	Angela walked outside.
She drank milk.	The doctor is busy.
He skates.	The pets are sleeping.
The cow has spots.	Horses and sheep are noisy.
He heard a bird.	Grandma likes biscuits and gravy.
The grass is green.	Don't spill your milkshake.
Clean your room.	It's fun to ride a bicycle.
She has brown eyes.	Carrots are a healthy snack.

#50665—Purposeful Play for Early Childhood Phonological Awareness

Words Around a Circle

Purpose

To segment sentences into words

Overview

The teacher asks children to memorize a sentence. Then, children segment it into individual words by taking turns saying the words in sequence around a circle.

Materials

Procedure

1. Have children sit in a circle, and tell them they will play a memory game. Their task is to remember a sentence. Ask them to listen carefully as you say a short sentence, such as, "I like lions." Have children repeat the sentence several times—to you, to their neighbors, and to themselves. Ask volunteers to repeat the sentence individually. Sample sentences are shown on the next page.

2. Tell children they may say only one word in the sentence as they go around the circle. Model the process: share the first word in the sentence—"I"—and then ask the group, "What's the next word?" Assist children in identifying the second word. Continue around the circle, saying one word at a time. If there are more children in the circle than there are words in the sentence, start the sentence again and continue to rotate around the circle.

3. Provide additional practice with the same sentence, starting with new volunteers each time. Then try different sentences. Use short sentences at first, followed by longer sentences.

4. Let children contribute their own ideas for sentences. Provide sufficient practice with each sentence so that all children can remember it.

Home Connection

Write one of the sentences for children to take home and share with their families. Perhaps they will want to play Words Around a Circle at home.

Modify or Extend

- Ask children to change a sentence they have memorized. For example, after saying "I like lions" around the circle, invite them to change *lions* to *tigers* or other words of their choice.

Words Around a Circle (cont.)

Sample Sentences

Single-Syllable, Multisyllabic, and Compound Words
Let's play outside.
I like to paint.
I have a dog.
The basketball is flat.
Panda bears eat bamboo.
We must clean our aquarium.
The little red hen baked bread.
Darrin rode his bicycle to school.
We had cereal for breakfast.
My neighbor grows tomatoes.

Standard: Children discriminate among the sounds of spoken language.

Robot Speak

Purpose

To blend words into sentences; to segment sentences into words

Overview

The teacher and children pretend to be robots, moving mechanically around the room and speaking to each other robotically by pausing between words in sentences. This silly game helps children notice that their speech is made up of individual words.

Materials

12-inch foil squares (one per child); tape; scissors; hole-punch; rope, twine, or ribbon (for constructing hats [*optional*])

Procedure

1. Tell children that you are going to pretend to be a robot. Walk in a stilted (robot-like) manner around the room. Say "I—am—a—robot," pausing between each word. Say other sentences, such as "I—want—a—crayon," or "I—need—to—sit—down."

2. Acting as a robot (pausing between words), provide directions for children to follow. Children will have to put words together in order to understand the directions. For example, say, "Touch—your—toes." Repeat the directions without pausing between the words, then ask children to perform the action. Share more directions as if you were a robot and wait for children to perform the actions. Sample sentences are presented on the next page.

3. Include opportunities for children to respond to you as robots.

4. Encourage children to give directions to their peers using Robot Speak. Play Robot Speak for as long as it holds the children's interest.

5. Find other opportunities throughout the day to use Robot Speak.

⌐Home Connection¬

Encourage children to speak like robots with their families. Sending home a prop, such as a foil hat, may spark their use of Robot Speak.

Modify or Extend

- Some children may spontaneously segment their speech into syllables. Help them recognize the difference between words and syllables.

- Make foil hats with children so they can wear them as they move and talk like robots. (Directions are shown on the next page.)

- If available, place toy robots at a center to prompt children's spontaneous use of Robot Speak in play.

Robot Speak (cont.)

Sample Sentences

Teacher Models	Call-and-Response
Walk—to—the—door. Pat—your—head. Touch—your—toes. Hop—on—one—foot. Move—like—a—robot.	Say, "I—am—a —robot." (Children respond, "I—am—a—robot.") Say, "I—like—to—play." (Children respond, "I—like—to—play.") Say, "I—am—walking—around—the—room." (Children walk like robots and respond, "I—am—walking—around—the—room.")

Make a tinfoil hat:

1. Start with a 12-inch square of tinfoil, with the shiny side out.

2. Make a cut in the foil from one side to the center in a straight line.

3. Bend the foil with one side under the other to make a cone shape, leaving the shiny side showing. Place the cone-shaped tin foil hat on the head and adjust the fit by shaping the foil against the head.

4. Tape the cut you made in the foil securely closed.

5. You can punch holes in each side of the hat with a pencil, ball point pen or tip of scissors and place rope, twine, or ribbon through the holes and tie snugly under the chin.

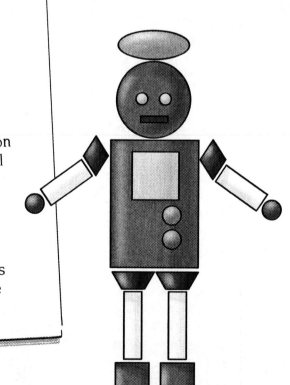

Guess My Word

Purpose

To blend words to produce compound words; to segment compound words

Overview

The teacher presents segmented compound words and children blend them to create a new word. Revisit this activity throughout the day, such as when children are putting on their jackets to play outdoors or cleaning up after a project.

Materials

picture cards of compound words available on the Teacher Resource CD (*optional*); markers or crayons (*optional*)

Procedure

1. Orally present two parts of a word, and ask children to put the parts together to create a new word.

2. Provide examples to ensure that they understand the task. For example, *news* and *paper* make *newspaper*. **Note:** At least one of the individual words in these compound words consists of more than one syllable. For example, *basket* in *basketball*. Compounds consisting of two single-syllable words such as *birth* and *day* in *birthday* are used in the Syllable Awareness section.

3. If you are using picture cards, reveal the corresponding picture after children have guessed the word. Then hand one card to each child. (Pictures may also be downloaded from the Internet, or found in magazines or other print media.)

4. After all cards are handed out, children can conceal the pictures and provide word part clues to help their classmates guess the words before revealing the picture.

Modify or Extend

- You may wish to model blending of these words by pausing between the two parts, then saying them closer together while bringing your hands closer together until you say them as a single word: *news—paper, newspaper.*

Home Connection

Have children draw a picture (or provide pictures) of any of the compound words you shared (or provide pictures). Practice saying the words in two parts, and encourage children to take the pictures home and play Guess My Word with their families.

Guess My Word (cont.)

Sample Compound Words

First Word	Second Word	Compound Word
baby	sitter	babysitter
basket	ball	basketball
butter	milk	buttermilk
candle	light	candlelight
grand	mother	grandmother
grass	hopper	grasshopper
news	paper	newspaper
sand	paper	sandpaper
sky	scraper	skyscraper
super	market	supermarket
table	cloth	tablecloth
thunder	storm	thunderstorm
waste	basket	wastebasket
water	melon	watermelon

Don't Say It!

Purpose

To delete words in compound words

Overview

The teacher asks children to say a compound word, then asks them to say it again with part of the word deleted.

Materials

picture cards of compound words available on the Teacher Resource CD (*optional*)

Procedure

1. Say a compound word and ask children to repeat it. If you have a picture card, show it to children.

2. Say the whole word again and tell children to repeat it, but this time they should remove one of its parts. Begin by deleting the first word in each compound. For example, tell children, "Say *motorboat* without saying *motor*." Children should respond with the word *boat*. Provide support as necessary.

3. If you are using picture cards, display several and invite a volunteer to select one and to say part of the word. Repeat until all cards have been used.

Modify or Extend

- After children have had many opportunities to delete the first part of the compound word, change the game and ask children to delete the second part of the compound. For example: "Say *firefighter* without *fighter*." Children should respond with the word *fire*.

Home Connection

Let children take home the picture cards to share with their families. Encourage them to say the full word, then to repeat just part of the word.

Don't Say It! (cont.)

Sample Compound Words

Compound Word	First Word	Second Word	Compound Word	First Word	Second Word
blackberries	black	berries	overcoat	over	coat
bulldozer	bull	dozer	rattlesnake	rattle	snake
butterfly	butter	fly	riverbank	river	bank
candlelight	candle	light	rubberband	rubber	band
cheeseburger	cheese	burger	sandpaper	sand	paper
coffeemaker	coffee	maker	skyscraper	sky	scraper
dishwasher	dish	washer	sunflower	sun	flower
fingernail	finger	nail	sunglasses	sun	glasses
firefighter	fire	fighter	supermarket	super	market
fireplace	fire	place	tablespoon	table	spoon
honeybee	honey	bee	thunderstorm	thunder	storm
ladybug	lady	bug	wastebasket	waste	basket
motorboat	motor	boat	waterfall	water	fall
motorcycle	motor	cycle	watermelon	water	melon
newspaper	news	paper	wheelbarrow	wheel	barrow

Standard: Children know that words are made up of sounds and syllables.

Five Little Monkeys

Purpose

To delete a target word from a song or chant

Overview

Using a repetitive chant, the teacher guides children to delete a target word each time it occurs in the chant. The teacher uses a gesture to signal the omission.

Materials

a variety of chants, such as the chant from the book *Five Little Monkeys Jumping on the Bed* by Eileen Christelow (1989) (*optional*)

Procedure

1. Teach the chant "Five Little Monkeys Jumping on the Bed" (share the book if you have it) and make sure children know it well.

2. Say the chant without the word *monkeys*. Instead, put your hand over your mouth each time the word should be spoken as a visual and kinesthetic reminder that a word has been omitted. Invite children to join you. **Note:** To avoid confusion, if you typically use other hand motions in this chant—holding up fingers as you count, putting your hand to your head, shaking your finger, miming a phone call—do not do so during this activity.

3. Say the chant again, and choose a different word to omit. Words that are used repeatedly, such as *bed*, *doctor*, and *Momma*, are good choices.

4. Have children suggest a word to delete.

Modify or Extend

- Rather than delete a word, have the children substitute a word. For example, chant about five little children or five little puppies jumping on the bed. Invite the children to suggest substitutions for other repeated words.

- Play this deletion game with other chants or songs children know. The table on the following page displays a list of several popular chants and songs in which words are used repeatedly. Melodies and lyrics can also be found on the Internet.

Home Connection

Encourage children to share the chant with their families. Suggest that they teach family members and others how to delete a word from the chant.

Five Little Monkeys (cont.)

Other Chants, Songs, and Rhymes

Chant	Word Repetition
"The Bear Went Over the Mountain" (Wells 1998)	bear, mountain, see, other, side
"The Wheels on the Bus" (Zelinsky 2000)	wheels, bus, round, town, swish, doors, open, shut, horn, beep
"Five Little Ducks" (Ives 2002)	ducks, hill, quack, mother, back
"It's a Small World" (Sherman and Sherman 1965)	world, share, small, all
"Mr. Sun" (Raffi 1996)	Mister, golden, sun, me, shine

"Five Little Monkeys Jumping on the Bed"

Five little monkeys jumping on the bed
One fell off and bumped his head
So Momma called the doctor and the doctor said,
"No more monkeys jumping on the bed!"
(repeat verse with four little monkeys, three little monkeys, and so on, until the last verse)
One little monkey jumping on the bed
He fell off and bumped his head
So Momma called the doctor and the doctor said,
"That's what you get for jumping on the bed!"

Word Awareness

Standard: Children know that words are made up of sounds and syllables.

Sentence Strips

Purpose

To segment sentences into words; to substitute one word for another

Overview

In this activity children understand that words are separate parts of a sentence by substituting individual words with pictures, then saying the sentence.

Materials

sentences written on tag board or poster board strips; picture cards; blank strips; scissors

Procedure

1. Write a simple sentence that ends in a noun in large print on a sentence strip. Substitute a picture for the last word. Point to each word as you read the sentence to children. Sample sentences are provided on the next page.

2. Ask children to point to each word and the picture as you read the sentence together.

3. As children say the first word in the sentence, cut the word off from the strip. Cut the remaining words off the strip one at a time. The picture will be the final piece. Place the pieces in order from left to right.

4. Have children read the sentence again and point to each piece. Bring out other pictures to substitute for the picture in the sentence. Display the alternatives, and name each one.

5. Ask a volunteer to replace the existing picture. Read the new sentence together, pointing to each word and the new picture as you say it. Repeat with additional pictures.

6. Introduce a second sentence strip and repeat the activity. Include sentences in which some printed words consist of more than a single syllable.

Modify or Extend

- Sentences should be simple and easily memorized. Do not expect children to recall the printed representation of individual words, although some may begin to do so through this exposure.

- Make the sentences available in packets that children may use later if they wish. Put one sentence strip and several pictures in each packet.

⌐Home Connection⌐

Provide children with a sentence strip to take home. Tell them they are welcome to cut the strip into words with their families. Or, provide them with a blank strip and invite them to work with an older family member to create a sentence to share with the class.

Sentence Strips (cont.)

Sample Sentences

Sentence	Alternative Picture Cards
I have a **_hat_**.	car, cat, cup, dog, spoon, watch, sweater, ring
My friend is [**_child's name_**].	photos of children
I like to **_swim_**.	play, sing, jump, climb, run, smile, eat
My friends and I can **_skate_**.	play, sing, jump, climb, run
I like to eat **_bananas_**.	apples, peaches, hamburgers, tacos, pizza, sandwiches
We are going to the **_market_**.	firehouse, post office, playground, beach, mountains, desert
I like the brown **_puppy_**.	cat, horse, hen, ball, sweater

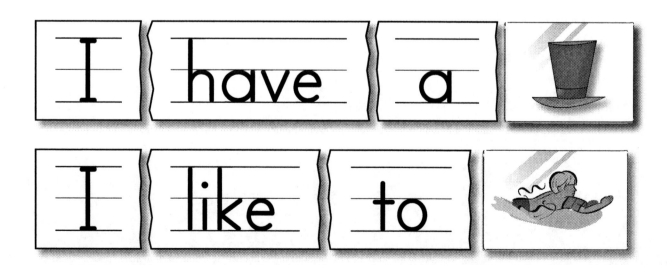

Syllable Awareness

Syllables are units of sound organized around a vowel sound. They are the beats in a word. *Rice* consists of one syllable, *pasta* consists of two, *burrito* consists of three, and *asparagus* consists of four. Young children typically find it easier to notice and manipulate syllables than smaller units of sound, such as onsets, rimes, and phonemes. However, the nature of the task, position of the sound, and amount of support will determine the relative difficulty of an activity. For example, matching words based on an initial phoneme is less challenging for most children than reversing the order of syllables in a word. Thus, some of the activities in this section are likely to be more difficult for young children than later activities that target smaller sounds.

In the next 12 activities, children are encouraged to perform a number of manipulations on syllables in playful contexts. Many of these syllable activities can be modified and used with onsets and rimes or phonemes at a later time.

Activity	Primary Task		
	blend	segment	delete
Have You Ever Heard Some Children?	x		
Clap, Clap, Clap Your Hands	x		
Bearsie Bear	x		
Dracula	x		
Count the Syllables		x	
Copycat	x	x	
Sort the Cards		x	
Syllable Turn Taking		x	
Cut It Apart		x	
Hide It		x	x
There Was a Teacher		x	x
Reverse!	x	x	x

Standard: Children know that words are made up of sounds and syllables.

Have You Ever Heard Some Children?

Purpose

To blend syllables into words

Overview

Using an adaptation of the song, "Have You Ever Seen a Lassie?" the teacher segments words into syllables and children blend the syllables together to create the words. At first, use compound words, and later use any two-syllable words. Children may generate their own words to be used in the song.

Materials

Have You Ever Seen a Lassie? by Bonnie Rideout (1998) (*optional*)

Procedure

1. Teach the song, "Have You Ever Seen a Lassie?" (If you are not familiar with the song, you can find it on the Internet or the Teacher Resource CD.) Make sure that children know it well. Ask children to help you create your own version of the song, replacing *seen a Lassie* with *heard some children*.

2. Sing, "Have you ever heard some children, some children, some children; Have you ever heard some children say this word with that?"

3. After you sing, "Say this word with that word," ask children to say the word that results from combining two words, such as *sun* and *shine*. Support them as necessary to respond *sunshine*. Provide several more segmented words and then sing the song again with new words.

Modify or Extend

- You may need to say the two parts a few times, making the pause shorter each time. Or hold and keep up one hand for *sun*, then the second hand for *shine* and move your hands together as you say *sunshine*.

- Extend this activity using two-syllable words that are not compound words. Instead of singing, "This word with that word," sing "This part with that part," or "This syllable with that syllable." Ask children to combine two syllables, such as /bā/—/bē/, then say the word *baby*.

- Some children may wish to lead the song. Recall that it is generally more difficult for children to segment a word than to blend a word that you have segmented into syllables. You may need to whisper two-syllable words for the leader to try.

⌐Home Connection⌐

Share this song with families, so they can sing it at home if they choose. Provide a list of two-syllable words. (See the table on the following page for suggested words.)

Have You Ever Heard Some Children? *(cont.)*

Sample Two-Syllable Words

Compound Words (each part is one syllable)	Noncompound Words
airplane	baby
backyard	candy
baseball	daisy
bedroom	finger
birthday	happy
cookbook	kitten
daylight	mother
football	music
jumprope	paper
moonlight	pencil
notebook	rabbit
outside	sandle
playground	student
sailboat	teacher
somewhere	window

"Have You Ever Heard Some Children?"

Have you ever heard some children, some children, some children,

Have you ever heard some children, say this word with that?

Say this word with that word,

Say this word with that word.

Have you ever heard some children, say this word with that?

Clap, Clap, Clap Your Hands

Purpose

To blend syllables into words

Overview

The teacher introduces the traditional version of the song "Clap, Clap, Clap Your Hands" and then changes the song to prompt children to blend syllables into words.

Materials

Procedure

1. Teach children the song, "Clap, Clap, Clap Your Hands." (If you are unfamiliar with the melody, you can find it on the Internet. Or, simply chant the lyrics.) Include corresponding movements.

2. Tell children you are going to add a new verse. You will sing "Say, say, say these parts," and their job is to put the parts together to create a new word. For example, if you say /pĭn/—/whēl/ (leaving a one-second pause between the two syllables in the word), they should say, "Pinwheel!" If you say, /tā/—/bəl/, they should say, "Table!"

3. Sing or chant the new verse. Children may sing along with the first four lines. Then provide a segmented word. The children respond with the blended word. Provide four different segmented words. Repeat the song with four new words.

Modify or Extend

- Two-syllable words work best with the beat of the song; however, you may decide to use words with more syllables.

- Some children may wish to assume the role of teacher and offer segmented words. Invite them to do so if they show an interest, and provide support.

Home Connection

Encourage children to share the song with their families. You may wish to provide a written copy of the lyrics and include a list of words. Invite them to bring a list of words of their choice (recorded by a family member) to use in the song with you and their peers.

Clap, Clap, Clap Your Hands (cont.)

Phonological Awareness Version

Teacher Says	Children Say
/moun/—/tən/	mountain
/ĕl/—/bō/	elbow
/frĕnd/—/shĭp/	friendship
/pō/—/nē/	pony

"Clap, Clap, Clap Your Hands"

Clap, clap, clap your hands,
Clap your hands together.

Clap, clap, clap your hands,
Clap your hands together.

Stomp, stomp, stomp you feet…

Shake, shake, shake your head…

Flap, flap, flap your wings…

Touch, touch, touch your toes…

Add the verse:

Say, say, say these parts,
say these parts together.

Say, say, say these parts,
say these parts together.

(Repeat song with four new words)

Standard: Children know that words are made up of sounds and syllables.

Bearsie Bear

Purpose

To add syllables to words (blending)

Overview

In *Bearsie Bear and the Surprise Sleepover Party*, the author adds ending syllables to animals' names, creating *Bearsie Bear*, *Cowsie Cow*, and *Foxie Fox*. The teacher points out the author's play with language and asks children to use the author's pattern to name several stuffed animals.

Materials

Bearsie Bear and the Surprise Sleepover Party by Bernard Waber (2002); small stuffed animals; small blanket or towel

Procedure

1. Read the book aloud and point out the author's language play, particularly the names of the characters.

2. Repeat the names of the characters. Encourage children to say them with you as you point to the animals in the illustrations.

3. Tell children that you have a collection of animals that would like to join the sleepover. Take one toy animal at a time out of a box or bag and ask children to identify it. Start with animals that have one-syllable names, such as a duck, bird, and cat.

4. Ask children what name they think the author of the book would give the animal. Guide them to say *birdie bird*. (*Birdsie Bird* is also acceptable. Notice that both /zē/ as in *Bearsie Bear* and *Cowsie Cow* and /ē/ as in *Foxie Fox* and *Piggie Pig* are used by the author.)

5. Set the animal on the blanket, and select another animal from the box or bag. Ask children to identify and name it.

Modify or Extend

- Place the animals in a center with the book and a small blanket, meant to serve as a bedspread. Children are likely to use the props to reenact and elaborate on the story.

⌐Home Connection⌐

Encourage children to bring a stuffed animal from home. Let them share their animals and tell one another the animals' names. Then ask them what Bernard Waber, the author of the book, might have named their animals.

Bearsie Bear (cont.)

#50665—Purposeful Play for Early Childhood Phonological Awareness

Dracula

Purpose

To add syllables to words (blending)

Overview

In this activity, children enjoy the poet's addition of *-ula* to the end of several words in the poem, such as *blackula*, *Cadillacula*, and *sackula*. The teacher models the addition of *-ula* to the ends of other words and encourages children to join in the language play.

Materials

"Dracula" from *Laugh-eteria* by Douglas Florian (2008)

Procedure

1. Read the poem aloud to children several times and encourage them to enjoy the word play.

2. Ask children what they noticed about some of the words in the poem. Guide children to hear /yo͞o/—/lŭ/ added to the end of many of the words. Repeat phrases or words and comment on several words. For example, note that the nonsense word *blackula* is really *black* with *-ula* added to the end.

3. Say your name with the addition of /yo͞o/—/lŭ/. Have children turn to peers and say their own names with /yo͞o/—/lŭ/ at the end. Support individuals as needed.

4. Have children say other words with the addition of /yo͞o/—/lŭ/. Say a familiar word (perhaps naming objects in the environment) and ask how Dracula would say it. For example, say *chair*. Children respond *chairula*.

5. Reread the poem and invite children to join in by saying the /yo͞o/—/lŭ/ words as you read them. Encourage children to add /yo͞o/—/lŭ/ to one another's names throughout the day.

Modify or Extend

- Share other poems that add sounds, such as Shel Silverstein's "Pinocchio" from *Falling Up* (1996) and Jeffrey Moss's "Ankylosaurus" from *Bone Poems* (1997).

⌐Home Connection⌐

Invite children to tell their families about the "Dracula" poem. Encourage families to share poetry with children. Ask them to send one of their child's favorites to school.

Dracula (cont.)

Excerpt from "Dracula"

by Douglas Florian (2008)

Hello, my name is Dracula.

My clothing is all blackula.

I drive a Cadillacula....

Standard: Children know that words are made up of sounds and syllables.

Count the Syllables

Purpose

To segment words into syllables; to count the number of syllables in words

Overview

The teacher reads aloud this story about Tikki Tikki Tembo, whose long name contrasts with that of his younger brother, Chang. The teacher and children repeat Tikki Tikki Tembo's full name as they clap and count the syllables. Then children clap and count the syllables in Chang's name and in their own names.

Materials

Tikki Tikki Tembo by Arlene Mosel (2007); drawing paper and supplies (*optional*); small squares of colored paper (*optional*)

Procedure

1. Read aloud *Tikki Tikki Tembo* by Arlene Mosel. Encourage children to try to say the very long name with you. Repeat it several times. Comment on its length.

2. Have children clap for each of the syllables in the name as you say it slowly. (You will clap 21 times!) Have children stand and stomp their feet for each syllable as you repeat the name again.

3. Ask children to clap the syllables in Chang's name. Comment on the difference between the two names.

4. Say your name and ask children to clap each syllable in your name. Discuss whether your name is more like Chang's or Tikki Tikki Tembo's in terms of its length. Then ask for volunteers to say their names and clap the syllables.

Modify or Extend

- Invite children to draw or paint a self-portrait. Then, have children take a piece of small colored paper to represent each syllable in their names. For example, Erica would take three papers, and Nha would take one. Each child glues a row of colored paper beneath his or her portrait. Portraits can be posted around the room or sorted by the number of syllables.

─Home Connection─

Invite children to bring photographs of their family members (or allow them to draw family members if photographs are not available) and clap the syllables in their names. Post the family pictures near the self-portraits.

Count the Syllables (cont.)

Amy

Jackson

Nha

Erica

#50665—*Purposeful Play for Early Childhood Phonological Awareness*

Standard: Children know that words are made up of sounds and syllables.

Copycat

Purpose

To segment words into syllables; to blend syllables into words

Overview

The teacher chants a copycat rhyme and then children repeat segmented words the teacher says. Later, children segment words on their own.

Home Connection

Encourage children to play Copycat at home with their families.

Materials

picture cards of multisyllabic words, available on the Teacher Resource CD (*optional*)

Procedure

1. Teach children the following chant:

   Copycat, copycat

   Say what I say.

   Copycat, copycat

   Please, won't you play?

2. Have children join you in reciting the chant. Then, say a word segmented into syllables. For example, say /rān/—/bō/ (*rainbow*), clearly separating the word's syllables. Ask children to copy you by repeating the word exactly the way you said it. Then ask if they can name the word. Support them as necessary.

3. Repeat the chant several times, using different multisyllabic words, such as *motorcycle*, *hamburger*, *mountain*, and *banana*. Use picture cards (available on the Teacher Resource CD), holding one up at a time as you use it in the chant. See suggestions on the next page.

Modify or Extend

- After children demonstrate that they can put syllables together, ask them to break a multisyllabic word into syllables. For example, if you say *hopscotch*, children would respond with /hŏp/—/skŏch/. Provide several examples, and then enjoy the game!

Copycat (cont.)

Sample Multisyllabic Words

Two Syllables		Three or More Syllables	
apple	mitten	applesauce	pajama
baby	peapod	banana	porcupine
butter	pencil	cantaloupe	radio
cactus	pizza	dinosaur	raspberry
candle	rabbit	elephant	referee
candy	raccoon	firefighter	restaurant
carrot	sandwich	hamburger	scorekeeper
chicken	sweater	hippopotamus	strawberry
crayon	tiger	kangaroo	sunflower
doctor	toothbrush	lightening	telephone
donkey	trumpet	lollipop	tornado
jacket	turtle	maximum	umbrella
kitten	water	medium	vehicle
lemon	yo-yo	national	yesterday
marker	zebra	newspaper	
	zipper		

Syllable
Awareness

Standard: Children know that words are made up of sounds and syllables.

Sort the Cards

Purpose

To segment words into syllables; to count the number of syllables in words

Overview

The teacher shares picture cards with children and asks them to identify the object pictured, then they count the number of syllables in the object's name. Children sort the cards according to the number of syllables in the object's name.

Materials

picture cards of objects that have one-syllable, two-syllable, and three-syllable names (available on the Teacher Resource CD)

Procedure

1. Share picture cards of familiar objects with children, or take digital photos of objects in the classroom or outside. Print the pictures and glue them to cardstock. Be sure children can identify the object on each card. (Sample pictures may be found on the Teacher Resource CD.)

2. Begin with an object that has either a one- or two-syllable name. Show the card and ask children to say the name of the object pictured. Together, count the number of syllables in the object's name. Encourage children to clap the syllables as they say the name. Continue to show cards and count syllables.

3. Have children help you sort the cards by number of syllables, perhaps by creating columns on the floor or in a pocket chart. Point to the cards in each group and name the cards together. Confirm that they are in the correct group.

4. Distribute the cards so each child has one. Let each child name the object on his or her card and then place it in the correct group of one-syllable or two-syllable objects.

Modify or Extend

- Begin with pictures of objects with one-syllable and two-syllable names. Later add pictures of objects with three-syllable names.

- Extend this activity by making cards available for children to use on their own.

⌐Home Connection ⌐

Encourage children to bring a picture of an object from home. Let them post their pictures on a wall or bulletin board, grouped by the number of syllables in the name of the object.

Sort the Cards (cont.)

Samples of Objects

One Syllable	Two Syllables	Three Syllables
ball	apple	apartment
bus	baby	banana
cat	carrot	computer
dog	doctor	crocodile
hen	jacket	dinosaur
horse	ladder	gorilla
key	lemon	motorhome
milk	paper	newspaper
moon	peanut	piano
mouse	rabbit	pineapple
nail	raccoon	potato
owl	sandwich	telephone
pen	table	tomato
rain	tiger	trampoline
ring	turtle	umbrella
shoes	wagon	violin
socks	yo-yo	
sun	zebra	
tree	zipper	

Syllable Turn Taking

Purpose

To segment words into syllables

Overview

The teacher and children segment a familiar nursery rhyme into syllables and take turns chanting the syllables.

Materials

copies of nursery rhymes for your reference (some are available on the Teacher Resource CD)

Procedure

1. Tell children you are going to take turns saying parts of a nursery rhyme with them.

2. First, recite together a familiar nursery rhyme, such as "Hickory, Dickory, Dock." When you are confident children know the rhyme well, ask them to say it without you. Then ask them to take turns saying the parts of the rhyme with you as call-and-response. For example, you say "Hickory, Dickory, Dock" and the children say, "The mouse ran up the clock," and so on.

3. Then, children alternate chanting the words in the rhyme with you or with each other. You say, "Hickory," the children say, "Dickory," and you say, "Dock." Take turns saying the words in the rest of the rhyme. (In this step, you are promoting word awareness.)

4. Tell children you are going to break the words into parts. Begin the rhyme by saying only the first syllable, /hĭk/. Children say /ə/, and you say /rē/. Alternate syllables as you recite the rhyme.

Modify or Extend

- Ask children to sit in a circle and recite the nursery rhyme syllable by syllable around the group. This will be more difficult because it requires individual responses rather than a group response. Allow children to support each other.

- Play this game again using different nursery rhymes. Suggested nursery rhymes are shown on the following pages.

Home Connection

Explain to families that you have been segmenting nursery rhymes and that these experiences are intended to increase children's awareness of the sound structure of the language. Invite them to share favorite nursery rhymes or poems from their childhood or cultural backgrounds. If they wish, after sharing with their children, they might try segmenting the rhymes as you did with "Hickory Dickory Dock."

Syllable Turn Taking (cont.)

Suggested Nursery Rhymes

"Humpty Dumpty"	"One Misty, Moisty Morning"
Humpty Dumpty sat on a wall. Humpty Dumpty had a great fall. All the king's horses And all the king's men Couldn't put Humpty Dumpty together again.	One misty, moisty morning, When cloudy was the weather, There I met an old man Clothed all in leather; Clothed all in leather, With cap under his chin. How do you do, and how do you do, And how do you do again!
"Diddle, Diddle, Dumpling"	**"Higglety, Pigglety, Pop!"**
Diddle, diddle, dumpling, my son John, Went to bed with his trousers on; One shoe off, and one shoe on, Diddle, diddle, dumpling, my son John.	Higglety, pigglety, pop! The dog has eaten the mop; The pig's in a hurry, The cat's in a flurry, Higglety, pigglety, pop!

#50665—Purposeful Play for Early Childhood Phonological Awareness

Standard: Children know that words are made up of sounds and syllables.

Cut It Apart

Purpose

To segment words into syllables

Overview

In this activity, children explore pictures of objects that have been cut into as many pieces as there are syllables in the object's name. Then, children cut pictures of other objects.

—Home Connection—

Invite children to take envelopes with picture pieces home to share with their families. Encourage children to bring their own pictures from home to share. Photocopy the pictures and cut them into as many parts as there are syllables in the words; then, add them to the class collection.

Materials

about 12 photos or illustrations of familiar objects, cut into as many pieces as there are syllables in the name of the object, and glued onto card stock with space between the pieces (see the next page for a sample); uncut pictures; card stock; scissors; glue; empty envelopes

Procedure

1. Show children the cards with the cut pictures. Help children identify the objects. (Pictures are available on the Teacher Resource CD.)

2. Tell children the pictures have been cut into pieces because words consist of parts. For example, show the picture of a tricycle cut into three parts, and say the word *tricycle* in three parts: /trī/—/sĭ/—/kəl/. Point to each picture part, starting from the left and moving right, as you say the syllables. Repeat the example a few times, inviting the group, then individual volunteers, to say the segmented words while pointing to their picture parts.

3. Share pictures that have not been cut. Identify one, say the word clearly and, as needed, emphasize the syllables. Ask children how many parts they hear in the word.

4. Model cutting the picture into the appropriate number of parts. Then glue the parts onto card stock so you can point to the picture parts left to right as you say the syllables and so the picture is still recognizable.

5. Allow each child or pairs of children to select a picture card to cut and glue. Support children to ensure success. Share all the cards children have developed with the group.

Modify or Extend

- Extend this activity by keeping cut pictures in envelopes. Allow children to remove the pieces from the envelopes and construct them into complete pictures.

Cut It Apart (cont.)

Sample Cut Picture

tri   cy   cle

Hide It

Purpose

To segment words into syllables; to delete the first or final syllable from words

Overview

In this activity pictures are cut into pieces (one piece for each syllable in the word) to help children delete syllables from words. Use this activity after children have played Cut It Apart (pages 72–73).

⌐Home Connection ¬

Invite children to take cut cards home to show their families. Some children will wish to share the picture parts and put them together like a puzzle as they say the object names. Others may wish to engage their families in the deletion activity. Encourage children to bring pictures from home to share, cut apart, and use in a deletion game with you.

Materials

picture cards that have been cut into pieces (one piece for each syllable in the word)

Procedure

1. Review the Cut It Apart activity with children. Select one picture and display its separate parts. Ask children to identify the picture and say its name, breaking the word into syllables. Point to parts as you say the syllables. For example, display a picture of an elephant that has been cut into three parts. Point to one part at a time as you say each syllable: /ĕl/—/ə/—/fənt/. Repeat this several times.

2. Tell children that you will turn one of the parts face down and together you will say only the parts that remain face up. Begin by turning the final syllable (fənt) face down. Point to the other two cards as you say the syllables /ĕl/ and /ə/. When you point to the overturned card, cover your mouth and say nothing.

3. Repeat this several times with other picture cards, encouraging children to join you.

Modify or Extend

- When appropriate, repeat the activity, but delete the first syllable instead of the final syllable.
- Make the cards available for independent play.

Hide It (cont.)

Sample Words

Two Syllables		Three or More Syllables	
apple	mitten	applesauce	porcupine
baby	peapod	banana	radio
butter	pencil	cantaloupe	raspberry
cactus	pizza	dinosaur	referee
candle	rabbit	elephant	restaurant
candy	raccoon	firefighter	storybook
carrot	sandwich	grocery	strawberry
chicken	sweater	hamburger	sunflower
crayon	tiger	kangaroo	telephone
doctor	toothbrush	lollipop	thermometer
donkey	turtle	magazine	tornado
jacket	water	newspaper	umbrella
ladder	yo-yo	octagon	vehicle
lemon	zebra	octopus	xylophone
marker	zipper	pajamas	yellowjacket

 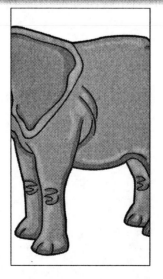 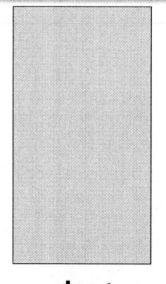

el   **e**   **phant**

Standard: Children know that words are made up of sounds and syllables.

There Was a Teacher

Purpose

To segment words into syllables; to delete syllables in words

Overview

The teacher shows children how to segment their names into syllables and then progressively delete syllables from their names as they sing a song. The deleted syllables are replaced by claps (as in the "B-I-N-G-O "song).

Materials

a variety of rhythm instruments (*optional*)

Procedure

1. Using the tune of "B-I-N-G-O," teach children the song shown on the next page using one of their names. (Search the Internet for "Bingo song" to hear the melody. Chanting the lyrics also works well.)

2. Tell children you are going to leave out one syllable from the name, but you will replace that part with a clap. Demonstrate, and ask children to join you.

3. Repeat the song again, and replace a second syllable with a clap or beat. Continue until all the syllables have been replaced by a clap or beat.

4. Ask children whose name they would like to try and continue singing as long as the activity holds the interest of children. The number of syllables in each child's name determines the number of verses in the song. A child named Claire will only need two verses—the first in which her name is used, and the second in which a single clap replaces the single syllable in her name. A child named Jose will have three verses—the first in which his name is used, the second in which a single clap replaces the first syllable of his name, and the third in which both syllables of his name are replaced with claps.

Modify or Extend

- If available, a variety of musical instruments can be used to rhythmically replace the syllables, enriching the singing experience. Children will enjoy using the instruments throughout the day and will likely play with segmenting other words and deleting syllables.

Home Connection

Encourage children to sing this song at home using the names of family members and friends. Or request from family members a list with the names of significant individuals in their child's life. Incorporate these names into the song on different occasions.

There Was a Teacher (cont.)

"There Was a Teacher" *(using the name Fernando)*

Verse 1:

There was a teacher who had a child.

Fernando was his name, oh!

/Fŭr/—/năn/—/dō/! /Fŭr/—/năn/—/dō/! /Fŭr/—/năn/—/dō/!

(pause between the syllables)

Fernando was his name, oh!

Verse 2:

There was a teacher who had a child.

Fernando was his name, oh!

CLAP—/năn/—/dō/! CLAP—/năn/—/dō/! CLAP—/năn/—/dō/!

Fernando was his name, oh!

Verse 3:

There was a teacher who had a child.

Fernando was his name, oh!

CLAP—CLAP—/dō/! CLAP—CLAP—/dō/! CLAP—CLAP—/dō/!

Fernando was his name, oh!

Verse 4:

There was a teacher who had a child.

Fernando was his name, oh!

CLAP—CLAP—CLAP! CLAP—CLAP—CLAP!

CLAP—CLAP—CLAP!

Fernando was his name, oh!

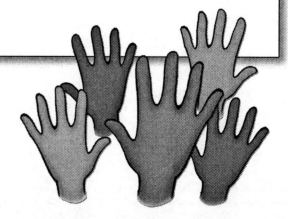

Reverse!

Purpose

To change the order of spoken syllables in two-syllable words (segment, delete, blend)

Overview

This activity engages children in reversing the order of the syllables in two-syllable words.

Materials

a list of compound and two-syllable words, available on the next page

Procedure

1. Ask children to turn on their "reverse switches." (This can be a twist of the nose or a tweak of the ears.) Ask children to try different activities in reverse, such as marching or walking. Have children sit in reverse (turning to face backwards). Tell them that next they will say words in reverse.

2. Ask two children to stand side by side. One says the word *cow* each time you gesture toward him or her; the other says the word *boy* at your signal. Gesture to the first child several times so you hear *cow, cow, cow.* Gesture to the other child: *boy, boy, boy.* Gesture back and forth: *cow, boy* (pause) *cow, boy.* Ask the children what word they hear (*cowboy*).

3. Tell children you are going to guide them to say the word *cowboy* in reverse. First, gesture to the child who says *boy,* then to the child who says *cow.* The result is *boy—cow,* or *cowboy* in reverse! Ask all children to say *boy—cow.*

4. Continue with additional words. Use compound words initially, such as those provided in the table on the next page.

Modify or Extend

- Challenge children by reversing the syllables in two-syllable words that are not compound words. For example, *mommy* (/mē/—/mŏm/), or *funny* (/nē/—/fŭn/).

- Include children's names that are two or more syllables. (*Kayla,* for example, becomes /Lə/—/kā/). Reverse your own name if it consists of two syllables.

┌ Home Connection ┐

Ask children to think of words they use at home with their families, and practice reversing the words. Encourage children to use the reversed words with their families that evening. For example, they might ask, "When is ner—din?" instead of "When is *dinner*?" and "May I have some cakes—pan?" instead of, "May I have some *pancakes*?"

Reverse! (cont.)

Sample Two-Syllable Words

Compound Words	Noncompound Words
airplane	candy
backyard	crayon
baseball	father
bathrobe	finger
bathroom	frighten
bedroom	happy
birthday	kitten
bookcase	mother
cookbook	mountain
daylight	music
football	paper
houseboat	pencil
jumprope	rabbit
moonlight	recess
notebook	student
outside	teacher
playground	
sailboat	
shipshape	
someday	
somewhere	

Onset and Rime Awareness

Onsets and rimes are *subsyllabic* (smaller than a syllable) units. The *onset* is the consonant sound or blend that precedes a vowel sound in a syllable, and the *rime* is the vowel sound(s) that follow it. In the word *stop*, /st/ is the onset because it precedes the vowel, and the rime is /ŏp/.

Rhymes are words with common rimes. In *cat* and *hat*, the common rime is /ăt/. There is currently insufficient evidence that rhyming activities, as traditionally conducted, contribute to the development of phonological awareness or learning to read. But, rhyming activities may serve as a springboard for drawing children's attention to the sounds of language. Furthermore, when conducted thoughtfully—with an understanding of the importance of building children's sensitivity to the sounds of language and clear explanations about the nature of rhyming words—these activities may be valuable.

The initial activities engage children in recognizing and generating rhymes; later activities focus on blending, segmentation, and deleting onset and rime.

Activity (*rhyming activities)	Primary Task					
	identify	match	blend	segment	delete	substitute
The Hungry Thing*	x	x				
The Hungry Thing Goes to a Restaurant*	x	x				
Rhymes in a Bag*		x				
Add a Verse*	x	x				
A Tisket, A Tasket*		x				
Hickory Dickory Dock*		x				
To Market! To Market!*		x				
Jamberry*	x	x				
Web of Words*		x				
The Ants Go Marching*		x				
I Spy			x	x		
The Mystery Bag			x	x		
Ring Around the Rosy			x	x		
Mail a Package			x	x		
Going on a Word Hunt			x	x		
I Say, You Say			x	x		
Trip! Trap!					x	
Puppet Play						x

Standards: Children know that words are made up of sounds.
Children know rhyming sounds and simple rhymes.

The Hungry Thing

Purpose

To identify and produce rhyming words (matching)

Overview

The teacher reads a book about a Hungry Thing who requests food by using rhyme to identify his wishes. This activity encourages children to listen carefully to rhyming clues and help identify what the Hungry Thing wants. After reading the book, the teacher produces a lunch bag and provides rhyming clues as to its contents. Children identify the items. Later they create their own lunch bags and provide rhyming clues to others.

Home Connection

Let parents or guardians know about your word play with food. Consider sending home the sample letter shown on the next page (and available on the Teacher Resource CD), and encourage families to enjoy the fun while they are eating at home.

Materials

The Hungry Thing by Ann Seidler and Jan Slepian (2001); lunch bags; real or plastic food items; pictures of food items, available on the Teacher Resource CD

crayons or markers, paper, and scissors (*optional*)

Procedure

1. Read aloud *The Hungry Thing* and have children predict the Hungry Thing's requests.

2. After enjoying the book, show children a lunch bag that contains three or four food items. Peek into the bag and give a rhyming clue for one of the items in the bag. The rhyming word can be a nonsense word. Encourage children to guess what you have. Withdraw the item from the bag and repeat the rhyming word and the real word pointing out the similarities in sounds. Provide rhyming clues for the remaining items, one at a time.

3. Distribute paper bags to children and invite them to select from a collection of several plastic or real food items to put in their bags. Have children circulate the room and provide rhyming clues for their classmates to guess which foods are in their bags. Give children the opportunity to consider the rhyming clue, think about what the Hungry Thing wants, and make their own guesses. For example, when he wants *fancakes*, pause before reading that *fancakes* are *pancakes*. **Note:** Use pictures of foods or let older children draw and cut out their own pictures of foods to place in their bags if the objects are not available.

Modify or Extend

- Keep bags and food items with the book at a center so children may revisit the book and continue their play with sounds as they wish.

The Hungry Thing (cont.)

Dear Parent or Guardian:

Today I read a book called *The Hungry Thing* by Ann Seidler and Jan Slepian. (Ask your child about this funny book!) Then, we played a game. Children guessed the names of common foods based on rhyming clues. For example, if I said I had some *napes*, children guessed that I had *grapes*. If I told them I had a *bandwich*, they guessed *sandwich*. Then, they created their own pretend lunches.

Playing with language is important because it increases children's sensitivity to the sound structure of our language—an important foundation for reading.

You can play this game at home. Ask your child if he or she would like you to pass the *deas* (*peas*) or offer to pour your child some *rilk* (*milk*). Then, let your child provide the silly rhyming words and see if you can figure out what he or she wants.

Play the game only as long as your child is interested, and have fun!

Sincerely,

_____

Queridos padres o custodio/a,

Hoy leí un libro que se llama *The Hungry Thing*, por Ann Seidler y Jan Slepian. (¡Pregúntele a su hijo/a que le diga sobre este libro cómico!) Luego jugamos. Los niños adivinaron los nombres de comidas comunes basado en pistas que riman. Por ejemplo, cuando yo les decía que tenía unas *tanzanas*, los niños adivinaron que tenía *manzanas*. Cuando yo les decía que tenía un *bándwich*, adivinaron *sándwich*. Luego, crearon sus propios almuerzos imaginarios.

Jugar con el lenguaje es importante porque aumenta la sensibilidad de los niños a la estructura del sonido de nuestro idioma—una fundación importante para leer.

Pueden jugar este juego en casa. Pregúntele a su hijo/a si a él/ella le gustaría que usted le pasara las *lapas* (*papas*) o ofrezca servirle *teche* (*leche*). Luego, haga que su hijo/a provea las palabras cómicas que riman y vea si usted puede averiguar lo que él/ella quiere.

Jueguen hasta que su hijo/a no tenga interés por jugar, ¡y diviértanse!

Sinceramente,

_____

Standards: Children know that words are made up of sounds.
Children know rhyming sounds and simple rhymes.

The Hungry Thing Goes to a Restaurant

Purpose

To identify and produce rhyming words (matching)

Overview

After sharing the book *The Hungry Thing Goes to a Restaurant*, in which a Hungry Thing orders food using nonsense words, the teacher shows children how to use rhyme to determine what the creature wants to eat.

Home Connection

Send sample take-out menus home with children, and encourage family members to talk about the menu selections. Children can pretend to order an item using rhyming words. Communicate to families with the letter on the next page. Remind families that their children should be familiar with the items they select.

Materials

The Hungry Thing Goes to a Restaurant by Ann Seidler and Jan Slepian (1993); plastic food items; serving trays; pictures of food items, available on the Teacher Resource CD (*optional*)

Procedure

1. Read *The Hungry Thing Goes to a Restaurant*. Ask children to identify what the Hungry Thing is ordering when they hear the nonsense rhyme. For example, when the Hungry Thing orders *bapple moose* to drink, children should say *apple juice*.

2. Show children a serving tray you prepared that contains a variety of food selections. Identify the items by briefly talking about each one. You pretend to be the Hungry Thing, and ask for volunteers to pretend to be servers. Request an item from the tray, using a nonsense rhyme. The servers, with their peers' assistance, identify the item and hand it to you. **Note:** If plastic foods are not readily available, you may use pictures of food from magazines or use the picture cards available on the Teacher Resource CD.

3. Offer children the opportunity to play the Hungry Thing. Provide rhyming clues as needed. Enjoy the activity, and laugh together about the silliness of the nonsense rhymes.

Modify or Extend

-   Make the materials and book accessible in a play area so that children may reenact the story and invent their own versions.

-   Place fewer or more items on the tray, depending on the children's ability to identify what you are requesting.

The Hungry Thing Goes to a Restaurant (cont.)

Dear Parent or Guardian:

Today I read a book called *The Hungry Thing Goes to a Restaurant* by Ann Seidler and Jan Slepian. (Ask your child about this funny book!) Then, we played a game. We pretended to be in a restaurant and we gave rhyming clues to tell our server what we wanted to order. For example, I wanted to order some apple juice, so I told children I wanted *bapple moose*.

Playing with language is important because it increases children's sensitivity to the sound structure of our language—an important foundation for reading.

You can play this game at home. Ask your child to provide rhyming clues to let you know what he or she would like for dinner. Then, you provide the rhyming clues and see if your child can guess what will be on the menu.

Play the game only as long as your child is interested, and have fun!

Sincerely,

_____

Queridos padres o custodio/a,

Hoy leí un libro que se llama *The Hungry Thing Goes to a Restaurant* por Ann Seidler y Jan Slepian. (¡Pregúntele a su hijo/a que le diga sobre este libro cómico!) Luego jugamos. Fingimos estar en un restaurante y dimos pistas que riman para decirle a nuestro mesero qué queríamos ordenar. Por ejemplo, yo quería ordenar jugo de manzana (apple juice en inglés), así que les dije a los niños que quisiera *bapple moose*.

Jugar con el lenguaje es importante porque aumenta la sensibilidad de los niños a la estructura del sonido de nuestro idioma—una fundación para leer.

Pueden jugar este juego en casa. Pídale a su hijo que provea pistas que riman para hacerle a usted saber qué le gustaría para la cena. Luego, usted provee las pistas que riman y vea si su hijo puede adivinar qué será en el menú.

Jueguen hasta que su hijo/a no tenga interés por jugar, ¡y diviértanse!

Sinceramente,

_____

Rhymes in a Bag

Purpose

To match rhyming words

Overview

In this activity, the teacher prepares two bags that contain rhyming objects. Children withdraw objects from one bag and match them with objects that are withdrawn from the second bag. Matching is based on rhyme.

Materials

pairs of rhyming objects; two bags

Procedure

1. Prepare for the activity by placing one object per rhyming pair in each bag. For example, put a rock in one bag and a sock in the other bag. (Sample items are shown on the next page.)

2. Ask children to withdraw objects from one bag. As each object is withdrawn, help children identify it by reviewing its name. Pronounce the name clearly, and ensure that children are using correct pronunciation. Have each child place the item they chose on the floor or table in front of him or her, where it can be easily seen by all.

3. Tell children that each object in the second bag rhymes with one of the objects they chose. Withdraw one of the items from the second bag.

4. Children decide if their item rhymes with the object from the bag. The child who has the rhyming object claims the second item and places it beside its match. Encourage all children to repeat the rhyming pair with you to confirm that they rhyme. Comment on the rhyming elements of the word pair.

5. Continue withdrawing items one at a time from the second bag until all items have been paired up.

Modify or Extend

- Share example and nonexamples of rhyming pairs. Ask children, "Would we be correct if we matched *cat* with *pail*? Do those words rhyme?"

- Have children search their indoor and outdoor environments to find additional rhyming pairs of object to place in the bags.

- Make the objects and the bags available for independent play.

⌐ Home Connection ⌐

Invite children to bring rhyming objects from home to place in the bag. If they cannot find two objects that rhyme, suggest they bring one object and you will work together to find an object that rhymes!

Rhymes in a Bag (cont.)

Sample Items

Bag 1	Bag 2
pail	nail*
book	hook*
cat	hat
bell	shell
jar	car
beads	seeds
dog	frog
moon	spoon
box	fox
house	mouse
coat	boat
sandal	candle
clock	rock
keys	peas
fan	man
ball	doll

*If item seems sharp, place it in
a sealed clear plastic bag.

#50665—Purposeful Play for Early Childhood Phonological Awareness

Standards: Children know that words are made up of sounds.
Children know rhyming sounds and simple rhymes.

Add a Verse

Purpose

To identify and produce rhyming words (matching)

Overview

Children learn the song "Down by the Bay." The teacher highlights the use of rhyme and encourages children to add new rhyming verses to the song. Children will enjoy laughing about the notion of a goose kissing a moose, a bear combing his hair, and so on.

Materials

Procedure

1. Teach children "Down by the Bay" (Raffi 1996), a rhyming song that lends itself to creating additional verses. (See the lyrics on the next page or on the Teacher Resource CD.)

2. Point out the rhyming element of the song and highlight rhyming pairs of words. Ask children to identify the rhyming words in some of the lines, such as, "Did you ever see a goose kissing a moose?"

3. Model adding a new verse to the song. For example, suggest, "Did you ever see an ant climbing on a plant?" Have the children identify the rhyming words.

4. Ask children to create verses. Provide prompts such as, "What might a cat do down by the bay?" Sing the song from the beginning and then ask children to add the new lines.

Modify or Extend

- Some children may spontaneously propose a phrase. Encourage responses, but provide prompts as necessary. For example, you may need to say, "What rhymes with *cat*? How about *hat*, or *rat*, or *bat*? What shall we choose?"

- Share other rhyming songs or chants that lend themselves to creating additional verses. Some examples are provided in the table on the next page

Home Connection

Encourage children to share the song with their families and invent more verses at home. If you have the technology available, record children singing and post their song on a class website, or burn and send home CDs.

Add a Verse (cont.)

Suggested Songs

Song	First Verse	Additional Verses
"Down By the Bay" (Raffi 1996)	Down by the bay Where the watermelons grow, Back to my home I dare not go. For if I do, My mother would say: **Did you ever see a bear combing his hair,** Down by the bay?	Did you ever see a goose kissing a moose… Did you ever see llamas eating their pajamas… Did you ever see a whale with a polka dot tail…
"My Aunt Came Back" (Cummings 1998)	My aunt came back **from old Japan,** And she brought with her a **big hand fan.**	…from old Algiers/…a pair of shears …from Holland too/…a wooden shoe …from Timbuctoo/…some gum to chew
"The Corner Grocery Store" (Raffi 1996)	**There was cheese, cheese, walkin' on its knees** In the store, in the store. **There was cheese, cheese, walkin' on its knees,** In the corner grocery store *Chorus:* My eyes are dim, I cannot see, I have not brought my specs with me. I have not brought my specs with me.	There were plums, plums, Twiddling their thumbs… There was corn, corn, Blowing on a horn… There were beans, beans, Trying on some jeans…
"Oh, A-Hunting We Will Go" (Langstaff 1991)	Oh, a-hunting we will go, A-hunting we will go; **We'll catch a little fox and put him in a box,** And then we'll let him go.	We'll catch a little squirrel and give it to a girl; We'll catch a little dog and put it on a log; We'll catch a little fish and put it in a dish;

Standards: Children know that words are made up of sounds.
Children know rhyming sounds and simple rhymes.

A Tisket, A Tasket

Purpose

To identify and produce rhyming words (matching)

Overview

As in the traditional game of the same name, children sit in a circle while one child skips around and places an item next to one of the children in the circle. That child uses a real or nonsense rhyming word to identify the object.

—Home Connection—

Using paper bags or shoeboxes, create individual "baskets" of items for children. Allow them to take the baskets home and make up rhyming words with their families. Or invite children to bring an object from home to place in the class basket the next day. Play the game again using the objects children brought from home.

Materials

a basket; small objects or picture cards; paper bags or shoeboxes (*optional*)

Procedure

1. Place small objects or picture cards in a basket, or ask children to gather some small objects from around the environment to place in the basket. (See the table on the next page for suggested items.) Be sure children are familiar with the items.

2. Have children sit on the floor in a circle. Select a child to carry the basket as he or she walks or skips around the outside of the circle while the other children sing the song, "A Tisket, A Tasket" (lyrics are available on the Internet).

3. At the conclusion of the song, the child carrying the basket removes an item and places it beside a child in the circle. That child identifies the object, places it in the center of the circle, and then states a rhyming word for it. Real and nonsense words are acceptable. For example, if the object is a pen, the child may offer *hen*, *ten*, or *Ben*, or nonsense words such as *fen*, *len* or *sen*. The first child sits down in the circle, and passes the basket to the new child, who repeats the process.

4. Continue the game as long as it holds children's interest. Objects may be used again.

Modify or Extend

- You may wish to invite every child in the circle to generate a rhyme for the object. Children may enjoy seeing how many rhymes the group can generate.

- Place the basket with the objects in an accessible place in the classroom so children can return to it and play the game on their own if they wish.

A Tisket, A Tasket (cont.)

Sample Objects for the Basket

Object	Possible Rhymes
block	lock, sock, zock
book	look, hook, vook
chalk	dalk, talk, walk
doll	ball, rall, tall
glue	do, new, shoe
mitten	bitten, kitten, vitten
pen	hen, nen, sen
rock	clock, dock, zock
tape	cape, nape, shape

#50665—Purposeful Play for Early Childhood Phonological Awareness

Onset
and Rime
Awareness

Hickory Dickory Dock

Purpose

To produce rhyming words (matching)

Overview

Children listen to and chant the nursery rhyme, "Hickory Dickory Dock." The teacher suggests changing some of the words in the poem and children use rhymes to create new lines.

Materials

paper (*optional*); markers or crayons (*optional*)

Procedure

1. Share the nursery rhyme "Hickory Dickory Dock." Help children learn the first verse shown on the next page. (The entire rhyme can be found on the Teacher Resource CD.)

2. Tell children you are going to change the poem. Rather than "Hickory Dickory Dock," you are going to say, "Hickory Dickory Dare." Ask children how you should complete the verse. Talk about rhymes and provide feedback to children's suggestions.

3. Change the rhyme to "Hickory Dickory Down." Begin to chant it, and encourage children to finish the verse. Try other versions, and encourage children to suggest other versions. Examples are included on the following page.

Modify or Extend

- Some children will quickly generate a rhyming phrase. Affirm that words rhyme when they do, and note—gently—when they do not. Return to the original version and draw children's attention to the rhyming words *dock* and *clock*.

- Record in writing some of the new rhymes and allow children to illustrate them. The rhymes and the illustrations may be displayed in the room and revisited occasionally.

⌐Home Connection⌐

Invite family members to share their favorite nursery rhymes. They may write them or teach them to their children to share orally with you. Create new versions of several of the rhymes, if children are interested. Or allow each child to illustrate the original and present it to his or her family.

Hickory Dickory Dock (cont.)

Additional Verses

Additional Verses	Rhymes
Hickory Dickory Dare,	...tripped on the stair; ...went to the fair; ...ran through my hair
Hickory Dickory Dig,	...became real big; ...ran to the pig; ...danced a jig
Hickory Dickory Done,	...ran in the sun; ...had lots of fun; ...ate a bun
Hickory Dickory Dip,	...ran up my hip; ...took a sip; ...was afraid to slip
Hickory Dickory Down,	...ran to the town; ...became a clown; ...made a frown

"Hickory Dickory Dock"
Hickory Dickory Dock,
The mouse ran up the clock.
The clock struck one,
The mouse ran down!
Hickory Dickory Dock.

To Market! To Market!

Purpose

To produce rhyming words (matching)

Overview

The poem "To Market! To Market!" makes playful use of rhyme. In this activity, the teacher shares a modified version of the rhyme with children. After they have learned it, the teacher prompts them to revise it by including different items that can be purchased at the market.

Materials

To Market! To Market! by Peter Spier (1992)
actual food items, plastic items, or pictures of food items from the Teacher Resource CD (*optional*)

Procedure

1. Share the rhyme "To Market! To Market!" with children. After children know the rhyme well, comment on and emphasize the rhyming words. Point out that the author changed *jiggity jig* to *jiggity jog* to create a rhyme for *hog*.

2. Change one of the words and ask children to try to complete the rhyme. For example, rather than saying, "To market, to market, to buy a *fat pig*," chant "To market, to market, to buy *some whole milk*." Say the new version and pause after the words, "*Home again, home again, jiggity*…" in the second line.

3. Have children complete the phrase. Some will create the rhyme (*jilk*); others may need your help. Be enthusiastic about children's attempts. Repeat the phrase with the new rhyme and encourage children to chant it with you.

4. Ask children what else they might find at the market and create the rhyme together. Recite the poem again, using different items that families might purchase at a market. Encourage participation. Some examples of market items with the corresponding rhyming phrase are presented on the next page.

Modify or Extend

- Have children select items or pictures of food from a collection and modify the rhyme in accordance with what they selected.

┌Home Connection┐

Ask families to look in their refrigerators and pantries with their children and identify items that came from a market. Then substitute the items into the rhyme. Or, ask families to send in empty food containers and recite the poem again using the items.

To Market! To Market! (cont.)

Sample Food and Rhymes

New Word	Rhyme
To market, to market, to buy…	Home again, home again…
cornbread	jiggity jed
whole milk	jiggity jilk
fine grapes	jiggity japes
yellow corn	jiggity jorn
green peas	jiggity jeas
string beans	jiggity jeans
wheat noodles	jiggity joodles
wild rice	jiggity jice
sweet butter	jiggity jutter
strawberries	jiggity jerries
sweet pears	jiggity jears
sliced cheese	jiggity jeese

"To Market! To Market!"

To market, to market, to buy a fat pig,
Home again, home again, jiggity jig;
To market, to market, to buy a fat hog,
Home again, home again, jiggity jog;
To market, to market, to buy a plum bun,
Home again, home again, market is done.

Jamberry

Purpose

To identify and produce rhyming words (matching)

Overview

The teacher reads a silly rhyming story about a boy and a bear who discover a variety of berries (some real, some not). Children invent berries of their own and create new verses for the book

⌐Home Connection⌐

Find out whether any families grow berries at home. If they do, invite them to share the process of how to grow berries, to bring in pictures of their berry plants, or even to provide some actual berries if they are in season. Send home a berry jam recipe so families who would like to do so can make their own berry jam.

Materials

Jamberry by Bruce Degen (1990); chart paper; markers or crayons; variety of berries (*optional*)

Procedure

1. Read aloud *Jamberry*. Enjoy the rhythm and rhyme of the story.

2. Read the story again and ask children which berries they think are real and which are make-believe. On chart paper, write "Real Berries" and "Imaginary Berries," and list their responses in the appropriate columns. Ask children if they know why the author created imaginary berries (to provide rhyming words and for simple enjoyment of the nonsense).

3. Have children invent berries. Look around the room or outdoors for ideas. Add children's ideas to the chart.

4. Share again some pages from the book. Suggest a new verse, such as: "Hatberry catberry I want a flat berry." Direct children's attention to the rhyming words.

5. Return to the chart and name the new berries children contributed. Suggest they use some of those berries to create their own new verses. For example, say "Look, we said floorberries!" and then add, "I want some more berries!" Or, say "Treeberries," followed by, "Give them to me, berries!"

Modify or Extend

- Consider rereading the pages on which the author used numbers: "One berry, two berry, pick me a blueberry," and encourage children to follow the counting pattern.

- Have children provide illustrations, and compile the pages into a book.

- Bring in a variety of berries to sample (check for food allergies first) and have children use rhyming language as they eat the berries.

Jamberry (cont.)

Sample Berries

Verse	Rhyme
One berry, two berry	... pick me a true berry
Hat berry, cat berry	... I want a flat berry
Floor berry, store berry	... I want some more berry
Tree berry, gee berry	... give them to me berry
Sun berry, fun berry	... I want to run berry
Nine berry, ten berry	... see the funny hen berry

Standards: Children know that words are made up of sounds.
Children know rhyming sounds and simple rhymes.

Web of Words

Purpose

To produce rhyming words (matching)

Overview

Web of Words should be played after children have had many opportunities to hear and talk about rhymes in books, songs, and poems. The purpose of this game is to generate as many rhymes for a word as possible as a skein of yarn is tossed from child to child.

Materials

a skein of yarn

Procedure

1. Sit in a circle with children. Tell children you are going to play a rhyme game. Remind them that rhymes are words that sound alike at the end and provide examples.

2. Begin the activity by holding a skein of yarn and saying a word, such as *dog*. (See the table on the next page for some other rhyming word ideas.) Ask if anyone can share a rhyme for your word.

3. Hold the end of the yarn, and gently toss the skein to a child who offers a rhyme.

4. Have the child hold onto his or her part of the yarn and toss the skein to another child who provides another rhyme for the word.

5. A yarn web is formed as the skein is tossed from child to child. When children can generate no more rhymes, congratulate them on the many words they generated. Then, suggest they begin a new round. Offer the word *kick*. Have children continue building the web with a new set of words. Make sure that every child has the opportunity to participate and hold part of the yarn.

Modify or Extend

- Use this game to focus on initial sounds instead of rhymes. Toss the yarn as words beginning with the same sound are generated (*big, blue, baby, boy, bike, beet, bake, boat, banana*). This activity targets phoneme awareness.

Home Connection

Encourage families to play rhyming games at home.

Web of Words (cont.)

Sample Rime Families

-ack	back, crack, jack, pack, quack, rack, sack, tack, whack
-ail	bail, fail, hail, jail, mail, nail, pail, quail, rail, sail, tail, wail
-at	bat, cat, fat, gnat, hat, mat, pat, rat, sat, that, vat
-ay	clay, day, fray, hay, jay, lay, pay, ray, say, tray, way
-ice	lice, mice, nice, price, rice, slice, twice
-ick	brick, chick, kick, lick, pick, quick, sick, thick
-ig	big, dig, fig, jig, pig, rig, twig, wig
-ight	bright, fight, light, might, night, plight, right, sight, tight
-ill	bill, chill, drill, fill, grill, hill, pill, skill, will
-in	grin, pin, shin, thin, win
-ip	chip, dip, flip, grip, hip, lip, rip, sip, tip, whip, zip
-og	bog, clog, dog, fog, hog, jog, log, smog
-op	cop, hop, mop, pop, shop, top
-ow	blow, crow, flow, glow, low, mow, row, show, tow
-ug	bug, drug, hug, jug, mug, plug, rug, slug, tug
-un	bun, done, fun, none, pun, run, stun, sun

Standards: Children know that words are made up of sounds.
Children know rhyming sounds and simple rhymes.

The Ants Go Marching

Purpose

To produce rhyming words (matching)

Overview

The teacher and children sing and march to the song, "The Ants Go Marching." After becoming familiar with the song, children invent their own rhyming lyrics.

Materials

Procedure

1. Teach children one or more verses of the song "The Ants Go Marching" (sung to the tune of the American Civil War song, "When Johnny Comes Marching Home"). The lyrics to the first verse can be found on the next page, and the complete lyrics are on the Teacher Resource CD.

2. Have children march around the room as they sing. Depending on which verse you sing, have children march single file ("one by one"), with a partner ("two by two"), with two partners ("three by three"), and so forth. Ask them to invent new rhymes to complete the lines. For example, in the first verse, the original lyrics are, "The little one stops to have some fun" (rhyming with "marching one by one"). What else might they sing to rhyme with "one"?

3. Have children bend their knees to get lower and lower as they sing the line, "And they all go marching down into the ground," while continuing to march. They should stand upright to begin the next verse.

Modify or Extend

- Provide part of a line that includes all but the rhyming word (see samples on the next page). For example, sing, "the little one stops to stand in the /s/…." Children complete the sentence with a rhyming word. Offer the initial sound of a rhyming word if children need extra support.

- Share one phrase that rhymes, and one that does not. Ask children to select the phrase that is appropriate for the song. Help them as needed to determine which phrase rhymes, and then sing and march with the new phrase.

Home Connection

Encourage children to share this marching song with their families. Find out whether any of the families have recordings of marching songs at home and invite them to share the recordings with the class. Or, ask whether families know other counting songs with rhymes and invite them to teach those to children.

The Ants Go Marching (cont.)

Sample Rhymes

Verse	Rhymes
one by one	...to stand in the sun ...to eat a bun ...then starts to run
two by two	...try something new ...say "ah-choo" ...to play "guess who"
three by three	...to chase a bee ...to jump with glee ...to tap his knee
four by four	...to go to the store ...to sing some more ...to clean the floor
five by five	...to dance a jive ...to swim and dive ...to say, "I'm alive!"
six by six	...to dig with sticks ...to light candle wicks ...to build with bricks
seven by seven	...to pray to heaven ...to play with Kevin ...to count to eleven
eight by eight	...to close the gate ...to stay up late ...to sit and wait
nine by nine	...to sort and combine ...to sit and dine ...to pay a fine
ten by ten	...to sing again ...to write with a pen ...to chase a hen

> **"The Ants Go Marching"**
>
> The ants go marching one by one.
>
> Hurrah! Hurrah!
>
> The ants go marching one by one.
>
> Hurrah! Hurrah!
>
> The ants go marching one by one;
>
> The little one stops to have some fun.
>
> And they all go marching down into the ground
>
> To get out of the rain.
>
> Boom, boom, boom, boom!

Onset and Rime Awareness

Standards: Children know that words are made up of sounds.
Children know rhyming sounds and simple rhymes.

I Spy

Purpose

To blend onsets and rimes into words; to segment words

Overview

In I Spy, the teacher spies an object in the room or outdoors and does not tell children what it is. Instead, the teacher provides a clue by segmenting the name of the object into onset and rime units. Children identify the object by blending the segmented units.

Materials

cardboard spyglasses made from empty toilet paper rolls or rolled paper; *Each Peach Pear Plum* by Janet and Allan Ahlberg (2004)

Procedure

1. Read *Each Peach Pear Plum*, a book in which well-known story or nursery rhyme characters are hidden in the pictures on each page.

2. Tell children you are going to play "I Spy." They will be detectives and use clues to figure out what you spy. Provide each child with one or two cardboard tubes (such as empty toilet paper rolls) or rolled paper to serve as a spyglass or binoculars.

3. Think of an object with a one-syllable name, either indoors or outdoors, that is within children's line of vision. (See suggestions on the next page.) Tell children, "I spy with my little eye something that sounds like this: ...." Finish the statement by providing the name of the object segmented into its onset and rime. Have children blend the units together to figure out what you spy. For example, you might say, "/r/—/ŭg/." Children respond, "Rug!" Provide feedback, explaining why a response is correct

Modify or Extend

- Extend this activity by only providing the onset. If the word is *shoe*, say "I spy something that starts like this: /sh/." Or make the rime the clue. If the word is *doll*, say, "I spy something that ends like this: /ôl/."

- Some children may want to try providing clues. Support them, as needed, perhaps even whispering the clue for them to share with their peers.

─Home Connection─

Encourage children to play I Spy at home with their families. Send home the spyglasses.

I Spy (cont.)

Sample Objects

Sound Units	Blended Word
/b/—/o͝ok/	book
/d/—/ĕsk/	desk
/fl/—/ăg/	flag
/g/—/ām/	game
/h/—/o͝ok/	hook
/m/—/ăp/	map
/p/—/ĕn/	pen
/s/—/ănd/	sand
/sl/—/īd/	slide

© Shell Education   #50665—Purposeful Play for Early Childhood Phonological Awareness

Standards: Children know that words are made up of sounds.
Children know rhyming sounds and simple rhymes.

The Mystery Bag

Purpose

To blend onsets and rimes into words; to segment words

Overview

The teacher places familiar objects in a mystery bag, then reaches into the bag, selects one object, and provides a segmented word clue before withdrawing it. Children blend the segmented parts of the word together to identify the object the teacher has selected.

⌐Home Connection⌐

Invite children to select one of the objects to place in a bag to take home to share with family members. Children should return their bags and objects the next day and then take a different bag and object home to share. Encourage children to take home different bags and objects over the course of one or two weeks.

Materials

familiar objects with single-syllable names; large paper bag; small bags for children to take home

Procedure

1. After sharing several familiar objects, have children place them in a mystery bag. (See the table on the next page for examples.)

2. Tell children that you are going to select one object from the bag but you won't show them what it is. Instead, you will ask them to guess the object you select based on a clue—the object's name broken into two parts. Model by withdrawing one item, such as a piece of string, and saying that your clue is /str/—/ĭng/. If they put the parts together they get the word *string*.

3. Select another object from the bag, and before withdrawing it, provide the segmented word clue.

4. If children guess correctly, withdraw the object to show them they were correct and repeat the segmented and blended forms of the word. If children are unable to guess or they guess incorrectly, repeat the clue and then withdraw the correct object and a second object. Say, "/gr/—/āps/. Is it the grapes or the doll?" Continue the guessing game until you have withdrawn all of the objects.

Modify or Extend

- Provide each child with an object in a bag. Encourage children to provide the segmented word clue for peers to guess what is in their bags.

- Periodically review the onset-rime segmentation of the names of the objects.

- Make the bag and objects available for later play.

The Mystery Bag (cont.)

Sample Objects

Object	Onset-rime Segmentation
boat	/b/—/ōt/
string	/str/—/ĭng/
doll	/d/—/ôl/
pen	/p/—/ĕn/
grapes	/gr/—/āps/
dress	/dr/—/ĕs/
man	/m/—/ăn/
clip	/kl/—/ĭp/
milk	/m/—/ĭlk/
ring	/r/—/ĭng/
bead	/b/—/ēd/
shell	/sh/—/ĕl/
book	/b/—/ŏok/
spoon	/sp/—/ōon/
plate	/pl/—/āt/

#50665—Purposeful Play for Early Childhood Phonological Awareness

Standards: Children know that words are made up of sounds.
Children know rhyming sounds and simple rhymes.

Ring Around the Rosy

Purpose

To blend onsets and rimes into words; to segment words

Overview

The teacher sings "Ring Around the Rosy" using different actions, such as crawling or jumping, but names each action by segmenting the word into its onset and rime. Children blend the word parts to determine and perform the action.

Materials

a list of words for reference

Procedure

1. Teach children the song and actions for "Ring Around the Rosy." (A version of the song is provided on the next page.) Have children sing the song as they walk or skip in a circle holding hands. On the final line, they drop their hands and all fall down.

2. After children have played, tell them to hold hands and walk or skip in a circle but instead of falling, you will tell them what to do in a silly way—as a broken word. For example, if you want them to jump, you will say "/j/—/ŭmp/!" If you want them to stomp their feet, you will say, "/st/—/ŏmp/!" (Suggested actions are presented in the table on the next page.)

3 Begin the song in the traditional way, singing and walking or skipping around in a circle. Provide the clue in the third line by segmenting a one-syllable word into its onset and rime. On the final line, have children say the word (with your help if needed) and then perform the action.

4. Repeat the song using a number of different actions.

Modify or Extend

- Encourage the children to suggest different actions. As needed, modify the segmentation clue to suit the action. For example, if a child offers a two-syllable word (such as *curtsey*), either segment the word into its initial sound and then the remainder of the word (/k/—/ûrtsē/), or into syllables (/kûrt/—/sē/).

- Try segmenting words into phonemes instead of onsets and rimes.

- Have children provide the segmentation clues.

Home Connection

Ask children to teach their families the game. Encourage them to return to school with additional actions to use.

Ring Around the Rosy (cont.)

Sample Actions with Onset-rime Clues

Action	Onset-rime Clue
clap	/kl/—/ăp/
crawl	/kr/—/awl/
cry	/kr/—/ī/
fly	/fl/—/ī/
hop	/h/—/ŏp/
jump	/j/—/ŭmp/
run	/r/—/ŭn/
scratch	/scr/—/ăch/
sleep	/sl/—/ēp/
stomp	/st/—/ŏmp/
stretch	/str/—/ĕch/
swim	/sw/—/ĭm/
yawn	/y/—/awn/

"Ring Around the Rosy"

All: Ring around the rosy,

A pocket full of posies,

Ashes, ashes

We all fall down!

All: Ring around the rosy,

A pocket full of posies

Teacher: /kl/—/ăp/, /kl/—/ăp/

All: We all will clap! (*all clap*)

Standards: Children know that words are made up of sounds.
Children know rhyming sounds and simple rhymes.

Mail a Package

Purpose

To blend onsets and rimes into words; to segment words

Overview

Children pretend to mail picture cards by slipping them into a cardboard mailbox. However, they may not slip their card into the box until the teacher asks for it. The teacher asks for the card by segmenting the name of the object into onset and rime units. Children chant a rhyme between each mailed card.

Materials

picture cards of objects with one-syllable names (see table on the next page or the Teacher Resource CD for examples); box that has a slot cut in it

Procedure

1. Distribute picture cards. Have each child show his or her card to a peer and then name the object pictured. (Make sure that each child knows the name of the object.)

2. Teach children the "Mail a Package" chant (see the next page). Have children pretend to mail a package to a friend that contains the item pictured on their card.

3. Ask children for the packages by saying the name of the object in segmented parts. For example, if the package contains a vase, you ask for a /v/—/ās/. Model chanting the rhyme and then ask for one of the picture cards by saying the object's onset and rime units. Then have the children slip the appropriate card into the mailbox. Model until you are sure children understand the game.

4. Continue to ask children for their cards by segmenting the names. Repeat until all children have mailed their packages. Leave the mailbox and the word cards in a center so children can play Mail a Package independently.

Modify or Extend

- Ask children if they have ever received a package in the mail and discuss the concept of mailing a package.

- Some children may want to try segmenting the words themselves. Allow anyone who wishes to do so to provide the onset-rime clues for the item to be mailed. Provide support as necessary.

⌐Home Connection⌐

Children can make their own mailboxes and take home picture cards. Encourage them to teach their families the chant and to play Mail a Package at home.

Mail a Package (cont.)

Sample Picture Cards and Onset-rime Units

Picture	Onset-rime Units
ball	/b/—/ôl/
blocks	/bl/—/ŏks/
cup	/k/—/ŭp/
flag	/fl/—/ăg/
hat	/h/—/ăt/
ring	/r/—/ĭng/
ship	/sh/—/ĭp/
train	/tr/—/ān/

"Mail a Package"

A package! A package!

What can it be?

A package! A package!

I hope it's for me!

#50665—Purposeful Play for Early Childhood Phonological Awareness

Standards: Children know that words are made up of sounds.
Children know rhyming sounds and simple rhymes.

Going on a Word Hunt

Purpose

To blend onsets and rimes into words; to segment words

Overview

Using a chant about going on a word hunt, students repeat each line after the teacher. Then, the teacher says a one-syllable word, segmenting its onset and rime. Children repeat the segments. Together, the teacher and children blend the onset and rime and announce the word.

Materials

cardboard tubes; glue; *We're Going on a Bear Hunt* by Michael Rosen and Helen Oxenbury (1997)

Procedure

1. Prepare for this activity by identifying some single-syllable words that have onsets and rimes to use in the chant. Words might include *mop, rain, friend, soap, nest,* and *zoo*. **Note:** Words with onsets that have continuant sounds (those that can be stretched and held over a period of time) are most useful for this activity. Noncontinuant sounds will not work as well. (See the table on the next page.)

2. Read aloud *We're Going on a Bear Hunt*. Talk about the story. Glue two empty cardboard tubes side by side to make binoculars. Go on a bear hunt by marching in a single file line around the room or yard. Chant lines from the book.

3. Tell children that you are going on a word hunt. Ask children to sit on the floor with their knees up and their feet flat on the floor. They will be tapping their toes and their knees.

4. Teach them to chant the words with a steady beat while they alternately tap their toes and their knees. When children blend the word, elongating the onset, they slide their hands from their toes to their knees and then complete the word (/mmmmm/—/ŏp/, *mop*).

Home Connection

Send the binoculars home with children so they can go on bear hunts with their families. They might want to go on word hunts, too!

Modify or Extend

- Provide pictures of objects named in the chant and have children select one to draw or glue onto a piece of paper. Help children segment the name of the object and then say the segmented word to a friend to guess the name of the picture.

- Support word awareness by using compound words, or syllable awareness by using two-syllable words. You may also highlight phonemes by using two-phoneme words, such as *on, up,* and *no*.

Going on a Word Hunt (cont.)

Sample One-syllable Words

Select Continuant Sounds	Words
/f/	fan, fence, fix
/l/	lake, lip, love
/m/	map, mint, mop
/n/	nap, nest, net
/r/	rain, read, ring
/s/	salt, sea, soap
/z/	zap, zip, zoo

"Going on a Word Hunt"

Teacher:	Going on a word hunt!
Children:	Going on a word hunt!
Teacher:	What's this word?
Children:	What's this word?
Teacher:	/m/—/ŏp/
Children:	/m/—/ŏp/
All:	/mmmmmmm/—/ŏp/
All:	Mop!

Standards: Children know that words are made up of sounds.
Children know rhyming sounds and simple rhymes.

I Say, You Say

Purpose

To blend onsets and rimes into words; to segment words

Overview

The teacher segments one-syllable words into onsets and rimes, engaging children in a chant. Then, children blend the segments together to announce the word. Hand motions are used so the oral blending is accompanied by the physical movement of hands coming together in a clap.

Home Connection

Encourage children to teach this chant to their families. Consider sending home a list of words segmented into their onsets and rimes so families can support their children as they segment and blend onsets and rimes.

Materials

Procedure

1. Say one part of a word, and tell children they will say a different part. Then they will put the two parts together to make a word.

2. Chant the lines and follow the directions on the following page. After chanting the first two lines, use both hands to point to yourself and say the onset. Then, extend both hands toward children as they say the rime. Repeat the word parts, pointing again to yourself with both hands and then extending both hands toward children. Let children say the entire word as you bring your hands together in a clap.

3. Get a rhythm going with the chant and repeat it several times with different words. See the table on the next page for examples of single-syllable words.

Modify or Extend

- Practice with a few words, explicitly talking about the word parts and then blending them together. Allow children to lead the chant and support them in segmenting words as needed.

- Start by inserting a long pause, then shorten the pause between the onset and rime as you model saying the two parts closer and closer together until they are blended into a single word.

- Make this a syllable blending activity by using two-syllable words.

I Say, You Say (cont.)

Additional Words

Onset and Rime Units	Blended Word
/bl/—/ŏk/	block
/fr/—/ŏg/	frog
/f/—/ōn/	phone

"I Say, You Say"

Teacher: I say "/st/" (*point to self*), you say "/ŏp/" (*point to children*)

Teacher: I say "/st/" (*point to self*), you say "/ŏp/" (*point to children*)

Teacher: /st/ (*point to self*)

Children: /ŏp/ (*point to children*)

Teacher: /st/ (*point to self*)

Children: /ŏp/ (*point to children*)

Teacher and Children: (*bring hands together*) Stop!

Teacher: I say "/r/" (*point to self*), you say "/ŭn/" (*point to children*)

Teacher: I say "/r/" (*point to self*), you say "/ŭn/" (*point to children*)

Teacher: /r/ (*point to self*)

Children: /ŭn/ (*point to children*)

Teacher: /r/ (*point to self*)

Children: /ŭn/ (*point to children*)

Teacher and Children: (*bring hands together*) Run!

#50665—Purposeful Play for Early Childhood Phonological Awareness

Standards: Children know that words are made up of sounds.
Children know rhyming sounds and simple rhymes.

Trip! Trap!

Purpose

To delete onsets in words

Overview

The teacher reads or tells the story of *The Three Billy Goats Gruff* in which three goats, one at a time, cross a bridge guarded by a troll. Using toy animals, children reenact the story in a modified way—as each animal "trip traps" across the bridge, the troll demands that it only say part of its name in order to pass.

Materials

any age-appropriate version of the book *The Three Billy Goats Gruff*; blocks or other objects to serve as a bridge; selected toy animals (see recommendations in the table on the next page); toy figure to represent the troll

Procedure

1. Read or tell children the story *The Three Billy Goats Gruff*.

2. Have children help you construct a bridge over which toy animals may pass. Next to the bridge, place a figure to represent the troll.

3. Show children a collection of animals that they know and can name, each of which wishes to cross the bridge. Select one animal and begin to move it across the bridge.

4. Ask a child to play the troll and say, "Who's that crossing over my bridge?" The troll will only permit the animal to pass safely if it can say its name without the first part (the onset). For example, a horse would say /ôrs/ and a frog would say /ŏg/.

5. Allow each child to select an animal to cross the bridge and help children name the animal when challenged by the troll. **Note:** Use only animal names that begin with a consonant sound or blend.

Modify or Extend

- Encourage the children to delete the onset of the words "Trip! Trap!" as they cross over the bridge. Guide them to say "Ip! Ap!" Try deleting the onsets from other one-syllable words.

- Keep the animals and the bridge materials at a center so children can revisit them as they wish.

Home Connection

Allow each child a chance to take home a copy of the book to share with his or her family, and to teach the game at home. You may also wish to invite children to bring their own toy animals to use with the game.

Trip! Trap! (cont.)

Sample Animal Names

Animal	Pronounced Without the Onset of the First Syllable
chicken	/īkən/
crocodile	/ŏkədīl/
crow	/ō/
donkey	/ŏngkē/
frog	/ŏg/
horse	/ôrs/
kangaroo	/ăngərōo/
pig	/ĭg/
sheep	/ēp/
skunk	/ŭngk/
snake	/āk/
squirrel	/ûrl/
swan	/ŏn/
zebra	/ēbrə/

#50665—Purposeful Play for Early Childhood Phonological Awareness

Puppet Play

Purpose

To substitute onsets in words

Overview

The teacher introduces a puppet, giving it a two-word name with both words beginning with the same onset. The puppet speaks its name and helps children say their own names with the same onset. Children listen to the puppet pronounce a variety of words, and those who wish are given a turn with the puppet.

Materials

puppets of any kind; socks or paper bags to make puppets (templates are available on the Teacher Resource CD) (*optional*)

Procedure

1. Select a puppet and give it an alliterative two-word name (so the onsets of the words are identical). For example, call a frog puppet *Freddy Frog*, call a ladybug puppet *Lizzie Ladybug*, or a snake puppet *Snazzy Snake*. If the puppet is a person, use names such as *Glad Glen*, or *Skippy Scott*. Point out that both words in the name begin with the same sound.

2. The puppet says everyone's name with the same beginning sound. Model with your name. Instead of Ms. H*olly*, Freddy Frog will say Ms. F*rolly*. Talk about the sound change.

3. Have the puppet say the names of several children. **Note:** Practice with children's names prior to implementing this activity so you can model the accurate substitution.

4. Invite a volunteer to hold the puppet. Encourage children to say other words with the target onset: bookcase/frookcase and sink/frink.

Modify or Extend

- Make the puppet available for later play so children can spontaneously engage in phonological play. Join individuals or small groups to support and extend their phonological play.

- Introduce different puppets on later days and repeat the naming activity.

Home Connection

Make sock or paper bag puppets with children that they may take home. Help children name the puppets, encouraging identical onsets as in this activity. Invite families to share puppets they may have.

Puppet Play (cont.)

Frog Puppet Template

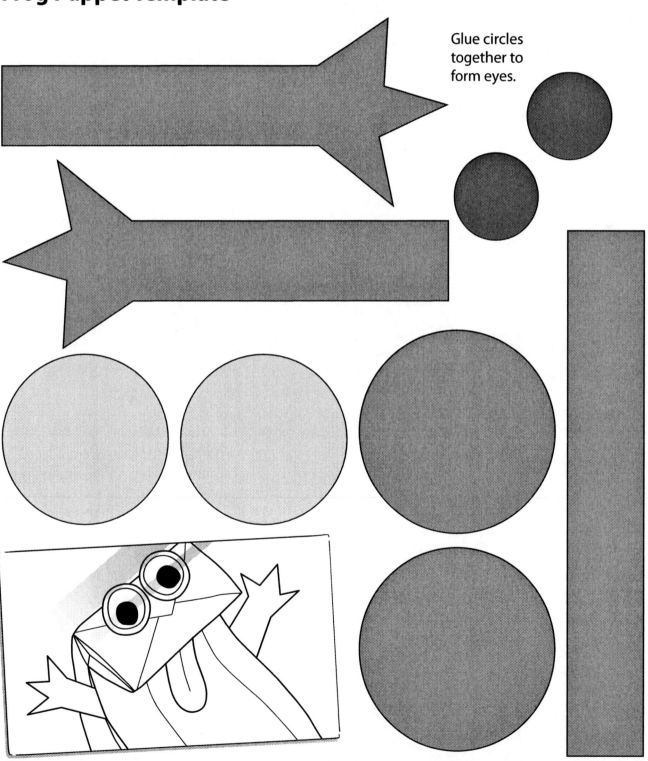

Glue circles together to form eyes.

#50665—*Purposeful Play for Early Childhood Phonological Awareness*

Phoneme Awareness

As we discussed in the introduction, phonemes are the smallest units of sound in spoken language. There are two phonemes in the word go: /g/—/ō/. There are three phonemes in the word run: /r/—/ŭ/—/n/. The word jump consists of four phonemes: /j/—/ŭ/—/m/—/p/. Research reveals that in order for children to appreciate the alphabetic principle—the fact that printed symbols represent the smallest sounds of speech in alphabet languages such as English—they must become phonemically aware. In other words, they must notice that speech consists of individual sounds. Our hope is that all children achieve phonemic awareness, the most advanced level of phonological awareness. Although we do not expect preschoolers to achieve full phonemic awareness, the early years are an optimal time to lay the groundwork for its development.

This section begins with activities that focus on the initial phonemes in words. These are likely the easiest activities in this section. It is interesting to note that, because most of these beginning activities involve words with single consonants in the initial position, the activities might also be considered onset activities. For example, /p/ is both the initial phoneme and the onset in *park*.

Activities presented later in this section are designed to build children's sensitivity to final or medial sounds in words. These and the activities that focus on blending, segmenting, deleting, and substituting sounds in words are more difficult. They require careful instruction and significant support. Some of the activities focus on substitution of initial phonemes. Thus, they might also be considered rhyming activities. They are included here, however, because the emphasis of the activity is the manipulation of the phoneme. It is the initial phoneme that is the object of attention. By contrast, activities that emphasize thinking of a word that sounds nearly the same as a target word—such as *fancakes* sounds like *pancakes* (see The Hungry Thing activity on page 82)—are placed with the rhyming activities in the Onset and Rime Activities section of this book.

Again, in the preschool years, the intention of phoneme-level instruction is to offer children exposure, not to expect mastery. It is important to ensure an environment in which phonemes are attended to, but demands for perfect performance are inappropriate.

Phoneme Awareness

	Activity	Primary Task					
		identify	match	blend	segment	delete	substitute
Initial Sounds	Sound Snacks	x					
	What Is My Word?	x					
	Do You Know?	x	x				
	Concentration	x	x				
	Willoughby Wallaby						x
	Cock-a-Doodle Moo!	x		x			x
	Sound Bingo	x					
	Pop! Goes the Weasel						x
	The Farmer in the Dell						x
	Head, Shoulders, Knees, and Toes						x
	Bappy Birthday Boo Boo						x
	Find Your Partner	x	x				
Initial and Final Sounds	The Golden Touch	x	x				
	Odd One Out!	x	x				
	The Line Game	x					
All Sounds	Can You Help Me with These Sounds?			x			
	If You Think You Know This Word			x	x		
	Turn It Over!			x			
	Segmenting Sam				x		
	Slow Motion Speech	x					
	Beginning, Middle, or End?	x			x		
	Elkonin Sound Boxes				x		
	Break It!				x		
	Simon Says					x	

#50665—*Purposeful Play for Early Childhood Phonological Awareness*

Standards: Children discriminate among the sounds of spoken language. Children know that words are made up of sounds.

Sound Snacks

Purpose

To identify initial phonemes in words

Overview

As a part of the snack routine, the teacher offers foods and beverages that target a particular sound. The teacher prompts children to note that all the snacks begin with the same sound. As children eat, they are encouraged to name other foods and words that begin with the same sound.

Materials

nutritious snacks that begin with a target sound; paper and drawing materials

Procedure

1. Select a target sound and food items that begin with that sound. For example, if you target the /b/ sound, provide snacks such as boysenberries, bananas, broccoli, and bagels. **Note:** Focus on the initial sound rather than the letter. Be especially careful if a vowel sound is targeted. *Oatmeal* begins with one sound made by the letter "O," but *olive* begins with a different sound.

2. Present the foods and ask children to identify them. Repeat the names of the items several times, emphasizing the initial sound for each. Assist children in noting that all begin with the same sound.

3. As children eat, talk about the foods and their initial sounds. Name other foods you might have included and ask children if they have suggestions of foods that begin with the same sounds.

Modify or Extend

- Invite children to draw pictures of the day's snacks and talk about their pictures. **Note:** Avoid writing the names of the items unless you are prepared to discuss the fact that different letters may represent the same sound. For example, *celery* and *soup* begin with the same sound. However, if they see the words, children may be confused by the fact that they begin with different letters.

Home Connection

Invite families to contribute snacks. Post or send home a sign-up sheet that provides a targeted sound and suggested snacks (to ensure that the snacks are healthy and that they begin with the appropriate sound). Encourage families to share foods from their respective cultural heritages.

© Shell Education

Sound Snacks (cont.)

Sample Snacks

Sound	Suggestions*
/b/	bagel, banana, bean dip, bean, beet, blackberry, blueberry fruit juice, boysenberry, bread stick, broccoli
/ch/	Cheerios, cheese, chicken, chili, chowder
/g/	graham cracker, granola bar, grapefruit, grape, green pepper, guacamole, guava
/k/	cabbage, cantaloupe, carrot, cauliflower, coconut, cookie, corn, corn tortilla, cottage cheese, couscous, cracker, cucumber, kiwi
/m/	macaroni, mango, mashed potatoes, melon, milk, mini shredded wheat, muffin
/p/	pancake, pasta, peach, peanut butter, pear, pea, persimmon, pineapple, pita bread, plum, pomegranates, popcorn, pretzel (whole grain), pudding
/r/	radish, raisin bread, raisin, raspberry, raspberry gelatin, red pepper, rice, rice cake
/s/	celery, cereal, salad, salsa, sandwich, smoothie, snap pea, soup, spaghetti, spinach, spring roll, sprouts, squash, strawberries, sunflower seed, sweet potato
/t/	tacos, toast, tofu, tomatoes, tortillas, turkey sandwiches
/y/	yams, yellow bell peppers, yogurt

*Always attend to choking hazards and be mindful of food allergies as you and children prepare and serve foods.

Standards: Children discriminate among the sounds of spoken language. Children know that words are made up of sounds.

What Is My Word?

Purpose

To notice and identify how phonemes are shaped in the mouth

Overview

This activity draws attention to how the shape of the mouth changes to make different sounds. The teacher tells children that he or she is going to say one of two words and asks children to guess the word based on the shape of his or her mouth. Children predict which word the teacher will say.

Materials

objects or picture cards from the Teacher Resource CD; mirrors (*optional*)

Procedure

1. Tell children they will guess which of two words you are about to say just by looking at the shape of your mouth.

2. Select two children whose names begin with different sounds. **Note:** Be sure their names begin with different enough sounds so that your mouth position noticeably changes. For example, the names *Peter* and *Billy* are too similar. *Peter* and *Ricardo* are a better contrast.

3. Children watch your mouth as you prepare to say one of the children's names. Children predict whose name you will say based on the shape of your mouth. After they respond, say the name.

4. Repeat each child's name several times, pausing between positioning your mouth and actually saying the name. Ask children to notice the shape your mouth takes for each name. Have children mimic what your mouth looks like.

5. Select a new pair of children and repeat the procedure. Allow children to take your role. Invite all children to prepare to say their own names without making a sound. Encourage them to look at each other's mouths. Provide mirrors so children can observe themselves making sounds and enjoy the silly faces!

Modify or Extend

- Use other targets, such as color words (*orange*, *blue*), number words (*two*, *five*), and topical words (*magnet*, *iron*).

- Hold two objects or picture cards, have children identify them, then have children turn to a partner and take turns positioning their mouths to say one of the words for their partner to guess.

⌐ Home Connection ⌐

Encourage family members to join their children in looking into a mirror as they pronounce words of their choice. You may wish to provide a small mirror for each child to take home.

What Is My Word? (cont.)

Standards: Children discriminate among the sounds of spoken language.
Children know that words are made up of sounds.

Do You Know?

Purpose

To identify initial phonemes in words; to match initial phonemes in words

Overview

The children sing the song, "The Muffin Man" and create additional verses that contain words that begin with the same sounds.

Home Connection

If you have books using alliteration in your library, allow children to take them home and enjoy them with their families. Also, ask families to share favorite tongue twisters, which often include alliterations, with their children and with you. If you have a class website, post several tongue twisters for families to view.

Materials

Procedure

1. Teach the song, "Do You Know the Muffin Man?" (The lyrics are provided on the next page and on the Teacher Resource CD.)

2. Have children form a large circle around one child. Ask them to hold hands and walk around in their circle as they all sing.

3. After singing, the child in the center chooses a partner from the circle to join him or her in the middle. These two now form a small circle and walk in the opposite direction of the outside circle as they all repeat the song.

4. Children continue to join the inside circle one at a time until all children have joined and no one remains in the outside circle. As the inner circle grows larger, children remaining on the outside will no longer be able to hold hands. They will walk around the inside circle without holding hands.

5. After children have played the game, help them notice that the words *muffin* and *man* begin with the same sound: /m/. Talk about alliterations and suggest others for the song. (See the table for examples.) Occasionally, suggest a lyric that is not an alliteration, such as *happy teacher*. Ask children why it is not a good choice.

6. Encourage children to create their own alliterations for the song.

Modify or Extend

- As children join the inner circle, have them suggest an alliteration for their own name for the next round of singing.

Do You Know? (cont.)

Additional Alliterative Lyrics

Sound	Verse
/b/	...the bitty baby
/k/	...the cuddly cat
/d/	...the dirty dog
/f/	...the funny farmer
/g/	...the giggly gardener
/l/	...the lily lady
/m/	...the merry mother
/p/	...the purple pig
/r/	...the red rhino
/s/	...the silly sailor
/t/	...the tiny turtle
/wh/	...the white whale

"The Muffin Man"

Do you know the muffin man, the muffin man, the muffin man?

Oh, do you know the muffin man who lives in Drury Lane?

Standards: Children discriminate among the sounds of spoken language.
Children know that words are made up of sounds.

Concentration

Purpose

To identify initial phonemes in words; to match initial phonemes in words

Overview

The teacher introduces a new version of the game Concentration, in which picture cards of objects beginning with two or three different sounds are placed facedown. One player turns over two cards. If the objects pictured begin with the same sound, the child earns the pair and takes another turn. If not, the cards are turned facedown and the next player has a turn.

⌐Home Connection⌐

Prepare sets of the picture cards for children to take home and use in play with their families. Or invite families to submit pictures beginning with target sounds.

Materials

picture cards (pairs of cards should begin with the same sound)

Procedure

1. Identify two or three sounds to target and select picture cards that depict objects that start with these sounds. **Note:** Be sure to have an even number of pictures for each sound. Use picture cards from the Teacher Resource CD, or find pictures from magazines or borrowed from other games or activities. Consider taking digital photographs of familiar objects and printing them for use in the game.

2. Explain how to play the game Concentration using the set of picture cards. Show children all of the cards that will be used and ensure that they recognize and can name the objects pictured.

3. Scramble the cards and place them facedown on a table or the floor. One player selects two cards to turn face up and names both of the objects pictured. If both begin with the same sound, the player keeps the two cards and takes another turn. The player continues until he or she selects two cards that do not begin with the same sound. The two cards are returned to their facedown position and the next child has a turn.

4. Play continues until all the cards have been taken.

Modify or Extend

- Start with highly contrasting sounds (such as /s/ and /m/) and later play the game with sounds that require finer discrimination (such as /b/ and /d/).

- Decrease or increase the number of cards or the number of sounds used in the game, depending on the children's level of success.

Concentration (cont.)

Sample Cards

/s/	/t/

Standards: Children discriminate among the sounds of spoken language. Children know that words are made up of sounds.

Willoughby Wallaby

Purpose

To substitute initial phonemes in words

Overview

Children sing the song "Willoughby Wallaby Woo" and playfully substitute the first sound in their names with the /w/ sound.

Materials

Procedure

1. Teach children the song "Willoughby Wallaby Woo." (The melody is available on the Internet, or chant the lyrics, shown on the next page.)

2. Sing the song again, but insert children's names and substitute the initial sound with the /w/ sound. Stop after several verses to ask children what they notice about the way the names are said. Repeat the names you have used and guide children to note that the sound at the beginning of each name is changed to a /w/ sound. Ask children to predict how other names would be said. For example, if you have not yet used the name LaToya, ask how that name would sound. Provide the phoneme substitution as needed: "LaToya would start with /w/. WaToya!"

3. Sing as many verses as necessary so each child hears his or her name in the song. Use your own name as well as the names of other significant individuals in the children's lives. **Note:** Some children may not wish you to use their names. Respect this.

Modify or Extend

- Return to the song on a different day or suggest another version using a different initial sound. Other versions might include Tilloughby Tallaby, Milloughby Mallaby, Zilloughby Zallaby, and so on. (See the chart on the next page.)

Home Connection

Encourage children to share this song with their families and to include the names of all family members and other important people.

Willoughby Wallaby (cont.)

Sample Lyrics for Different Initial Sounds

Sound	Verse
/s/	Silloughby Sallaby Soo...
/h/	Hilloughby Hallaby Hoo...
/z/	Zillougby Zallaby Zoo...
/m/	Millougby Mallaby Moo...

"Willoughby Wallaby Woo"

Willoughby Wallaby Woo,

An elephant sat on you.

Willoughby Wallaby Wee,

An elephant sat on me.

#50665—Purposeful Play for Early Childhood Phonological Awareness

Standards: Children discriminate among the sounds of spoken language.
Children know that words are made up of sounds.

Cock-a-Doodle-Moo!

Purpose

To identify sound units in words; to blend phonemes in words; to substitute initial phonemes in words

Overview

The teacher reads the book *Cock-a-Doodle-Moo!* in which a rooster wakes up to discover he cannot crow above a whisper. After several unsuccessful efforts to awaken the farm animals, the rooster enlists the aid of a cow. The result is a series of hilarious phoneme substitutions. Children then engage in sound manipulations of their own.

Materials

Cock-a-Doodle-Moo! by Bernard Most (1996); toy farm animals

Procedure

1. Read aloud *Cock-a-Doodle-Moo!* Encourage children to join in as they anticipate the /zzz/ added to the beginning of the animal sounds and the /haw/ added to the end of the sounds.

2. As you read, talk about the cow's attempts to crow *cock-a-doodle-doo.* Guide children to notice the sound substitutions.

3. Ask children to repeat the cow's efforts to *cock-a-doodle-doo.* Invite them to invent other ways the cow might have changed the phrase.

Modify or Extend

- Ask children about animals that are not mentioned in the book. How would a goat snore? (*Zzz-maa!*) A sheep? (*Zzz-baa!*) How would these animals awaken with a laugh? (*Maa-ha! Baa-ha!*) **Note:** Animal sounds offered by children will vary, especially if you have a culturally diverse group; all suggestions for animal sounds should be honored.

- Extend this activity with a story modification. What if a donkey tried to awaken the animals with a loud *hee haw*? What are some ways the cow might have incorrectly uttered *hee haw*? Perhaps *ree raw*? Encourage a variety of versions.

- Place toy farm animals at a center, along with the book. Provide time for children to visit the center for continued play with animal noises.

⌐Home Connection⌐

Invite children to bring toy animals from home. Retell the story using children's animals as story characters.

Cock-a-Doodle-Moo! (cont.)

Standards: Children discriminate among the sounds of spoken language. Children know that words are made up of sounds.

Sound Bingo

Purpose

To identify initial phonemes in words

Overview

Children each receive a game card with pictures of various objects. As the teacher says a sound, children find an object on their card that begins with that sound. They place a chip on the picture, and when they have three chips in a row, they exclaim, "Bingo!"

Materials

bingo picture cards (templates available on the Teacher Resource CD); chips (or other markers)

Procedure

1. Prepare sound bingo cards (use the blank templates from the Teacher Resource CD). All cards should target the same sounds, but no two cards should be identical. (See the sample card on the next page.)

2. Distribute the cards, keeping one for yourself, and make sure children can identify the objects pictured on their cards. Provide children with chips to mark their cards.

3. Children find an object on their cards that begins with the sound you call out. Model the task by saying a sound, such as /m/, and finding an object that starts with /m/ on your card. Name the picture, emphasizing the first sound. Place a chip on the picture. Ask children to share pictures on their cards that begin with /m/.

4. Play the game. Instruct children to say "Bingo!" when they have covered three pictures in a row, and continue playing until all pictures on children's cards are covered with chips.

Modify or Extend

- Allow children to work with partners, if they choose.
- You may wish to create a set of letter cards to draw from a bag. Share the sounds with children.

⌐Home Connection⌐

Send home bingo cards and chips with children so they can play Sound Bingo at home with their families. If you have a class website, you may wish to display cards that can be downloaded from the Teacher Resource CD.

#50665—Purposeful Play for Early Childhood Phonological Awareness

Sound Bingo (cont.)

Sample Sound Bingo Card

Standards: Children discriminate among the sounds of spoken language. Children know that words are made up of sounds.

Pop! Goes the Weasel

Purpose

To substitute initial phonemes in words

Overview

Children sing the traditional song, "Pop! Goes the Weasel" and play the accompanying game. The teacher focuses on the word P*op!* and substitutes the initial sound in the word with other sounds.

Materials

Procedure

1. Have children sit in a circle on the floor. Teach them the traditional song "Pop! Goes the Weasel." (The lyrics appear on the next page.)

2. Model the game for children by skipping or walking around the outside of the circle while singing the song. After you sing the third line, "The monkey thought it was all in fun," stop skipping, pause in your singing, and then sing the final line with a substitution for *pop*, such as *hop*, *mop*, or *lop*. Help children identify that you changed the first sound in the word.

3. Skip around the circle and sing again. Ask children to think of a different initial sound substitution for *pop*. Have children take turns skipping or walking around the circle. All the children sing the first three lines, but the child skipping says the word *pop* with a different initial sound. Then, everyone sings the last line with the new word.

4. Have the child rejoin the circle and select another child to skip around the circle. The game continues until all children have had a turn or until children are no longer interested.

Modify or Extend

- Review initial sounds and practice adding them to the /ŏp/ word.

- Ask children to use the initial sound in their own names to create a new /ŏp/ word. For example, a child named Sam would sing "S*op* goes the weasel." If a child's name begins with a vowel sound, add the vowel sound to the beginning of /ŏp/. For example, a child named Amy would sing, "A-*op*!"

Home Connection

Ask families to share traditional songs from their home cultures with the class. Only if appropriate, change the initial sound of one of the words in the song.

Pop! Goes the Weasel (cont.)

"Pop! Goes the Weasel"

All around the mulberry bush
The monkey chased the weasel;
The monkey thought it was all in fun,
Pop! Goes the weasel.

Standards: Children discriminate among the sounds of spoken language.
Children know that words are made up of sounds.

The Farmer in the Dell

Purpose

To substitute initial phonemes in words

Overview

Children sing and play the traditional song and game "The Farmer in the Dell." The teacher shows them how to change the initial phonemes in the phrase Hi-*ho, the derry-o* to form alliterations.

Materials

Procedure

1. Teach the traditional song and game "The Farmer in the Dell." (See lyrics on the next page and on the Teacher Resource CD.) Have children form a circle. One child plays the "farmer." The circle moves around the farmer as children sing the first verse.

2. As they sing the second verse, the farmer selects someone from the circle to join him or her as the "wife" (or spouse). During the third verse, the "spouse" selects someone to join them in the center as the "child," and so on. Finally, the "rat" chooses the "cheese." Everyone, except the child who is the "cheese," leaves the center to reform a circle around the "cheese," who stands alone. The "cheese" becomes the "farmer" for the next round.

3. Once students understand the game, change the lyrics so that instead of singing Hi-*ho, the derry-o*, you will sing Mi-*mo, the merry-o*. Ask children what they notice about the new lyrics. Guide them to observe the substitution and repetition of the /m/ sound.

4. Ask children to suggest other sounds to substitute in the phrase. Sing together and enjoy the sound manipulation.

⌐Home Connection⌐

Suggest that children teach their families the song and game. Ask which other versions of Hi-*ho, the derry-o* they plan to share. Invite them to return to class with more suggestions.

Modify or Extend

- Add children's names to the song and target additional words in the song for sound substitution using the child's initial phoneme. For example, "Nathan in the nell, Nathan in the nell, Ni-no, the nerry-o, Nathan in the nell."

- If children are familiar with some letters, select one, show it, talk about its name and sound, and make the appropriate substitution in the song.

The Farmer in the Dell (cont.)

Additional Sounds and Verses

Sound	Verse
/b/	Bi-bo, the berry-o
/d/	Di-do, the derry-o
/f/	Fi-fo, the ferry-o
/p/	Pi-po, the perry-o
/s/	Si-so, the serry-o

"The Farmer in the Dell"

The farmer in the dell,
The farmer in the dell,
Hi-ho, the derry-o
The farmer in the dell.

The farmer takes a wife,
The farmer takes a wife,
Hi-ho, the derry-o
The farmer takes a wife.

The wife takes a child,
The wife takes a child,
Hi-ho, the derry-o
The wife takes a child

(*additional verses*)
The child takes a nurse…

The nurse takes a cow…

The cow takes a dog…

The dog takes a cat…

The cat takes a rat…

The rat takes the cheese…

The cheese stands alone…

#50665—Purposeful Play for Early Childhood Phonological Awareness

Head, Shoulders, Knees, and Toes

Purpose

To substitute initial phonemes in words

Overview

Children sing the song "Head, Shoulders, Knees, and Toes," touching each body part as they sing about it. Then they substitute initial sounds in the song.

Materials

Procedure

1. Teach the song "Head, Shoulders, Knees, and Toes." (The lyrics appear on the next page and on the Teacher Resource CD, and the melody can be found on the Internet.) As children sing about each body part, have them touch it with both hands.

2. After singing the song in its original form several times, start the name of each body part with a different sound, such as /l/ (*lead, loulders, lees,* and *loes*). Sing with children, using the motions, and invite them to join in.

3. Talk about the sound changes. Ask what you might call your thigh if it was in the song. What about your ankle? cheek? fingers? Assist children as they substitute the initial sounds in these words and provide feedback.

4. Ask children if there is a different sound they would like to try. As needed, suggest sounds. Have fun!

Modify or Extend

- Sing the song faster each round. This will be especially challenging with the modified versions of the song. Provide ample practice prior to increasing the speed.

⌐Home Connection⌐

Encourage children to share the original and the silly versions of the song with their families. Later, ask them to share with you and their peers other ways their families sang the song.

Head, Shoulders, Knees, and Toes (cont.)

Sample Verses

Sound Substitution	Verse
/b/	bed, boulders, bees, and boes
/d/	dead, doulders, dees, and does
/f/	fed, foulders, fees, and foes
/j/	jed, joulders, jees, and joes
/k/	ked, koulders, kees, and koes
/l/	led, loulders, lees, and loes
/m/	med, moulders, mees, and moes
/n/	ned, noulders, nees, and noes
/p/	ped, poulders, peas, and poes
/r/	red, roulders, rees, and roes
/s/	sed, soulders, sees, and soes
/v/	ved, voulders, vees, and voes
/w/	wed, wolders, wees, and woes
/y/	yed, youlders, yees, and yoes
/z/	zed, zolders, zees, and zoes

"Head, Shoulders, Knees, and Toes"

Head, shoulders, knees, and toes,
Knees and toes
Head, shoulders, knees, and toes,
Knees and toes
Eyes and ears and mouth and nose

Head, shoulders, knees and toes,
Knees and toes!

(substitute the /l/ sound)
Lead, loulders, lees, and loes…

Standards: Children discriminate among the sounds of spoken language.
Children know that words are made up of sounds.

Bappy Birthday Boo Boo

Purpose

To substitute initial phonemes in words

Overview

With support from the teacher, children sing the traditional "Happy Birthday" song but they substitute the initial sounds in the lyrics with the initial sound of the birthday child's name.

Materials

Procedure

1. As appropriate, have children sing the "Happy Birthday" song to one another on their birthdays.

2. Change the song to match the first sound in the name of the child whose birthday you are celebrating. (See the table on the next page for examples.) Invite children to join you as you sing the silly version several times. **Note:** First determine whether this is culturally inappropriate or results in inappropriate words.

3. Talk about the phoneme substitution. Explain that when you replace the /y/ in *you* with an /m/, for example, the word is *moo!* Sing the song again. Allow the birthday child to select which version he or she would like to hear—the traditional version or the silly sound version.

Modify or Extend

- Instead of substituting initial phonemes in the song, have the children generate rhymes for the birthday child's name and add one or more rhymes to the song when the name is sung. For example, if the child's name is Dan, sing "Happy birthday, dear Dan man" or "Dan pan" or "Dan van fan man." Be sensitive to whether the birthday child is enjoying the silly play with his or her name and be attentive to the possibility of inappropriate rhymes.

Home Connection

Encourage children to tell their families about the birthday celebrations. Invite them to share the new version of the song with their families.

Bappy Birthday Boo Boo (cont.)

Sample Substitutions

Name	Initial Sound	Verse
Benjamin	/b/	Bappy birthday boo boo
Ethan	/ē/	E-appy Earthday e-oo e-oo
Franco	/f/	Fappy firthday foo foo
Gabby	/g/	Gappy girthday goo goo
Kathy	/k/	Kappy kirthday koo koo
Lea	/l/	Lappy lirthday loo loo

"Happy Birthday To You"

Happy birthday to you,
Happy birthday to you.
Happy birthday, dear _____,
Happy birthday to you!

Find Your Partner

Purpose

To identify initial phonemes in words; to match initial phonemes in words

Overview

The teacher gives each child an object or picture card to hold. Children say the name of the object, listening carefully for the initial sound. Then they find a partner who is holding an object that begins with the same sound.

Materials

a variety of objects or picture cards from the Teacher Resource CD; a box or other container to hold all the objects or cards

Procedure

1. Collect a variety of objects (enough for one for each child in the group) that can be sorted into pairs based on their initial sound, and place them in a box. **Note:** If there is an odd number of children in the group, have three objects that begin with the same sound available, or include yourself in the game so every child has a partner. The table on the next page shows suggestions, or picture cards may be used instead.

2. Have children each select an object from the box. Together, identify the objects.

3. Hold an object and ask children to say the object's name. Model how you identify the first sound you hear, then ask children to listen carefully as you repeat the word and emphasize the sound. Have them identify the first sound they hear when they say the name of the object.

4. After all the objects have been distributed, have children find partners who have objects that begin with the same sound as their objects. Have children decide together whether they can form a partnership. Ask each pair to show their matching objects. Comment on the matching of initial sounds, repeating the words with children and emphasizing the sound.

5. Have children return their objects to the box. Repeat the process.

Modify or Extend

- Initially, avoid using sounds that are very similar in the same round of the game. For example, /b/ and /d/ are more difficult to discriminate than /f/ and /m/. Later, include sounds that are similar.

⌐Home Connection⌐

Invite children to bring objects from home on another day and have them find an object in the room (or one brought in by a friend) that starts with the same sound. Or encourage them to pair objects they have at home based on initial sound.

Find Your Partner (cont.)

Suggestions for Object Pairs

Initial Sound	Object 1	Object 2
/b/	ball	block
/k/	cat	castanet
/d/	duck	dish
/f/	fork	firetruck
/h/	hat	horn
/l/	lemon	leaf
/m/	menu	mouse
/n/	napkin	necklace
/s/	sand	spoon
/sh/	shell	ship
/t/	tambourine	tub

#50665—Purposeful Play for Early Childhood Phonological Awareness

The Golden Touch

Purpose

To identify initial or final phonemes in words; to match phonemes

Overview

The teacher gives each child a plastic gold coin and a card that has three boxes, representing the beginning sound, middle sounds, and the ending sound of a word. Children identify whether a sound is at the beginning or the end of each word and place the coin in the appropriate box on their cards.

Materials

King Midas and the Golden Touch by Charlotte Craft (1999); one plastic gold coin for each child; card templates on which three connecting boxes are drawn (one card for each child; samples available on the Teacher Resource CD)

Note: The middle box is darkened because medial sounds are not addressed in this activity.

Procedure

1. Read aloud *King Midas and the Golden Touch*. Highlight the importance of the word *gold* in the story. Ask children to say the word *gold* several times. Emphasize the initial /g/ sound.

2. Provide each child with a gold coin and a card. Tell children to listen carefully as you say words that have a /g/ sound. If a word has the /g/ sound at the beginning, children put their gold coins into the first box on the card. If the word has the /g/ sound at the end, the gold coin is placed in the last box.

3. Say the word *gold*. Emphasize the initial sound. Help children understand that they need to place their gold coins in the first box on their cards.

4. Say the word *dig*. Emphasize the final sound. Help children understand that they need to place their gold coins in the last box on their cards.

5. Try other words from the table on the next page.

Modify or Extend

- Try this activity with other sounds. Use markers that begin with the target sound, if possible. For example, use small plastic dinosaurs when targeting the /d/ sound. Use small cubes when targeting /k/.

⌐Home Connection⌐

Incorporate family names, street names, and other important words in children's lives that begin or end with the target sound. Allow those who wish to share the activity with their families to take a card and marker home.

The Golden Touch (cont.)

Sample Words with /g/ Sound

Initial Position	Final Position
game	bag
gate	big
gear	dog
gift	flag
glow	fog
go	frog
goat	hog
golf	leg
goose	plug
green	rug

#50665—Purposeful Play for Early Childhood Phonological Awareness

Standards: Children discriminate among the sounds of spoken language.
Children know that words are made up of sounds.

Odd One Out!

Purpose

To identify initial or final phonemes in words; to match initial or final phonemes in words

Overview

Children play a game in which they identify the object or picture that does not belong with the others because it begins with a different sound.

Materials

objects or picture cards, such as those listed in the charts on the next page (available on the Teacher Resource CD)

Procedure

1. Organize a variety of objects or picture cards into sets of three. Two of each set should begin with the same sound and one should begin with a different sound.

2. Show children three objects and together name them. Tell children that objects go together if they begin (or end) with the same sound. Help children identify the odd object and remove it from the set.

3. Play the game with other sets of objects, targeting different initial or final sounds.

Modify or Extend

- Make the sets of objects available for later play.

- Target medial sounds after children have demonstrated an ability to match initial and final sounds.

⌐Home Connection ¬

Encourage children to share the game with their families. Ask families to send a few objects to school and use them for the activity. Or, send home picture cards in sets of three such that two go together and one is the odd one out.

Odd One Out! (cont.)

Sample Objects for Same Initial Sound

Objects	Same Initial Sound	Odd One Out
paper, pencil, key	paper, pencil	key
staples, book, banana	book, banana	staples
watch, wallet, penny	watch, wallet	penny
cup, key, tissue	cup, key	tissue
marble, tennis ball, marker	marble, marker	tennis ball
string, staples, hair clip	string, staples	hair clip
clip, key, brush	clip, key	brush
napkin, rubber band, ruler	rubber band, ruler	napkin
tissue, key, tennis ball	tissue, tennis ball	key
tape, tissue, brush	tape, tissue	brush
spoon, wallet, staples	spoon, staples	wallet
key, penny, paper	penny, paper	key

Sample Objects for Same Final Sound

Objects	Same Final Sound	Odd One Out
clip, cup, key	clip, cup	key
marble, pencil, book	marble, pencil	book
marker, paper, tissue	marker, paper	tissue
spoon, leaf, napkin	spoon, napkin	leaf
tape, rubber band, clip	tape, clip	rubber band

#50665—Purposeful Play for Early Childhood Phonological Awareness

The Line Game

Purpose

To identify initial and final phonemes in words; to match phonemes

Overview

This is a challenging activity and ample support should be provided throughout. Each child is provided a picture card. Children line up by matching their cards so the final sound of one child's card is the same as the beginning sound of the next child's card.

Materials

carefully selected picture cards, one for each child in the group (see the table on the next page for suggestions)

Procedure

1. Distribute the picture cards. Have children identify the objects pictured.

2. Select a child to start the line. Name the object pictured, and help children identify the final sound.

3. Have children look at the cards they are holding and decide if they have a picture that begins with the same sound as the ending sound on the first picture card. The child holding a picture that begins with that sound stands next in line.

4. Tell children the new object's name and identify its final sound. They continue to form a line using final and initial sounds until everyone with a card is standing.

5. Redistribute the cards and play the game again.

6. Try the game with another set of cards

Modify or Extend

- Consider taking and printing photographs of the line of children. Be sure the pictures on the cards are easily identifiable. Post an enlarged copy of the photograph so children may view it. When they look at themselves, they are likely to revisit the activity, pointing to the pictures and naming the objects.

- Make the sets of cards available for children to manipulate at a later time.

┌ Home Connection ┐

Invite children to draw or find pictures of objects at home and bring them to share. Select, as appropriate, some to use in a line game. If you have taken photographs of children holding the cards in a line, send them home with children to share.

The Line Game (cont.)

Sample Ideas for Picture Card Sets

Card Sets*	Sound Progression
1	tiger—rock—cup—plate
2	sun—nut—tub—book—car—rope—peas
3	cat—tape—polar bear—radio—oak
4	dinosaur—rabbit—table—leaf—frame—mad
5	soap—popcorn—nut—table—lake—caterpillar—rice

Sets should work in a circular way so that any card could be first.

Standards: Children discriminate among the sounds of spoken language. Children know that words are made up of sounds.

Can You Help Me with These Sounds?

Purpose

To blend phonemes in segmented words

Overview

The teacher asks children to help put together a word that has been segmented into its constituent phonemes using the tune of "Are You Sleeping?" Children reply by blending the phonemes to create the word.

Materials

picture cards (*optional*)

Procedure

1. Teach children the lyrics on the next page to the tune of "Are You Sleeping?" Conclude the song by sharing a segmented three- or four-phoneme word, such as /k/—/ă/—/t/.

2. Have children blend the phonemes and say the word *cat*. Offer guidance as needed. Restate the sounds and the word.

3. Provide more segmented words for children to blend. Repeat the song several times, using new segmented words each time. Suggested words are displayed in the table on the next page.

Modify or Extend

- Use the same song for blending syllables into words. For example, you sing /krŏk/—/ə/—/dīl/ and children say *crocodile*.

- Use picture cards to support the children. Display several cards and identify one of the objects pictured by saying it in segmented form. Have children select the picture card you named.

- For a more difficult task, invite children to take the lead and provide words in segmented forms for their peers to blend.

Home Connection

After children are comfortable with the song, and if they can segment several words themselves, invite them to take home a picture card as a prop to share the song with their families. Encourage them to find objects in their homes to sing about. Welcome them to bring those objects to share with the other children.

Can You Help Me with These Sounds? *(cont.)*

Sample Words

Three Phonemes	Four Phonemes
book	desk
cat	frog
dog	grass
hat	hand
look	jump
mice	school
moon	skip
night	wrist
play	
rug	
sit	

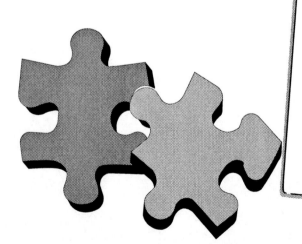

"Can You Help Me?"

Can you help me, can you help me,
With these sounds, with these sounds?
Tell me what the word is, tell me what the word is:
/k/—/ă/—/t/ (*children respond, "cat!"*)
/s/—/ŭ/—/n/ (*children respond, "sun!"*)
/t/—/ō/—d/ (*children respond, "toad"*)
(*repeat with other words*)

If You Think You Know This Word

Purpose

To blend phonemes in segmented words

Overview

Singing to the tune of "If You're Happy and You Know It," the teacher provides words that have been segmented into phonemes. Children blend the sounds to announce the word.

Materials

picture cards from the Teacher Resource CD (*optional*)

Procedure

1. Teach children the lyrics on the next page to the tune of "If You're Happy and You Know It." Children listen to the individual sounds of words and then blend the sounds together to form the words. For example, /k/-/ŭ/-/p/ is *cup* and /th/-/r/-/ō/ is *throw*. Provide support and feedback.

2. If you are using picture cards, select one and hold it so children cannot see the picture. Sing the song and provide the segmented word. When children respond, reveal the picture.

3. Repeat the song several times, using a variety of words.

4. As appropriate, invite children to offer their own segmented words. This is a more difficult task as children move from blending words that you have segmented to segmenting words themselves.

Modify or Extend

- Begin with two- or three-phoneme words. Later, share four-phoneme words.

- Use the same song for blending onsets and rimes or syllables into words.

- Support children by using words from a category that you announce. For example, tell them you will be singing about color words or number words.

⌐Home Connection⌐

Encourage children to share this new version of "If You're Happy and You Know It" with their families.

If You Think You Know This Word (cont.)

Sample Words

Two Phonemes	Three Phonemes	Four Phonemes
day	big	books
eat	bug	cats
go	cup	cloud
hi	cut	dogs
ice	duck	drum
me	fly	fence
off	good	frame
show	home	grass
up	hot	last
	juice	lift
	leaf	lunch
	ride	sand
	sun	

"If You Think You Know This Word"

If you think you know this word, say it now,

If you think you know this word, say it now.

If you think you know this word,

Then tell us what you've heard.

If you think you know this word, say it now.

(*teacher*) "/d/—/ŭ/—/k/" (*children respond*) "duck!"

(*teacher*) "/f/—/ĭ/—/sh/" (*children respond*) "fish!"

(*teacher*) "/h/—/ă/—/t/" (*children respond*) "hat!"

#50665—Purposeful Play for Early Childhood Phonological Awareness

Turn It Over!

Purpose

To blend phonemes in segmented words

Overview

The teacher shares several picture cards and names one in segmented form. Children blend the phonemes to form the word that identifies the correct picture, and then they turn the card face down.

Materials

picture cards (available on Teacher Resource CD)

Procedure

1. Collect or construct picture cards of objects with one-syllable names. Use the picture cards available on the Teacher Resource CD or from other print sources.

2. Place several picture cards in front of children. Identify each picture with children.

3. Name a picture by saying each of the phonemes in the word separately. Have children repeat the phonemes, and guide them to blend the sounds. If they can identify the correct picture, they turn the card face down.

4. Continue the game until all the cards have been turned face down.

5. Play again if children wish. Make the cards available for independent play.

Modify or Extend

- The first time you try the activity, use only a few cards with pictures that are quite different in terms of sounds (such as *cup* and *man*). As children gain experience, increase the number of cards and include some that have similar sounds (such as *bat* and *book*).

- Use the same activity with onset-rime and syllable units.

Home Connection

Invite children to take home several picture cards to share with their families. Some children may try segmenting the words. Others will just want to talk about the pictures.

Turn It Over! *(cont.)*

Sample Words

Two Phonemes	Three Phonemes	Four Phonemes
day	bug	cats
go	cup	dogs
ice	duck	frog
off	fly	glove
show	home	lamp
up	juice	lunch
	leaf	
	sun	

© Shell Education   #50665—Purposeful Play for Early Childhood Phonological Awareness

Standards: Children discriminate among the sounds of spoken language.
Children know that words are made up of sounds.

Segmenting Sam

Purpose

To segment words into phonemes

Overview

The teacher introduces a puppet named Segmenting Sam and invites children to share a word with Sam. Sam segments the word into its constituent phonemes and provides a good model of phoneme segmentation.

Materials

any puppet; picture cards (*optional*)

Procedure

1. Introduce children to the Segmenting Sam puppet. Sam can take any word and segment it into its separate phonemes, which means that he can say all the individual sounds in words. Demonstrate how Sam says the word *fish* and then says "/f/—/ĭ/—/sh/."

2. Ask a child to say a word to Sam. Have Sam repeat the word and then segment it into its phonemes. Continue playing, segmenting as many words as holds children's interest.

3. Have children take turns playing the role of Sam. Provide ample support so children segment the words correctly.

Modify or Extend

- Use the puppet periodically, including during transition times. Make the puppet available for children to use during the day in a variety of play settings.

- Provide a set of picture cards. (See suggestions for picture cards on the following page.) Children draw a card, identify the object, and Sam segments it.

Home Connection

Make simple puppets for children to take home. Invite them to play with the puppets however they wish with their families.

Segmenting Sam (cont.)

Sample Words

Two Phonemes	Three Phonemes	Four Phonemes
day	big	brush
eat	bug	cats
go	cup	dress
hi	cut	grape
ice	duck	hand
me	fly	last
off	good	lift
show	home	lunch
up	hot	sand
	juice	sink
	leaf	swim
	ride	
	sun	

#50665—Purposeful Play for Early Childhood Phonological Awareness

Standards: Children discriminate among the sounds of spoken language.
Children know that words are made up of sounds.

Slow Motion Speech

Purpose

To identify the phonemes in words

Overview

The teacher models speaking very slowly so that phonemes are exaggerated and become more noticeable. Children are encouraged to speak in slow motion, too.

Materials

small, plastic "walking" spring toys (*optional*)

Procedure

1. Ask children to move in slow motion. Suggest several actions, such as waving, turning around, flapping their arms, or putting on a hat.

2. Start to speak in slow motion, stretching words as you say them. Begin with your name. Say it very slowly. Have children say it. Then, have children say their own names in slow motion to themselves and to a partner.

3. Say other words in slow motion. (See the next page for sample words.) If you have a plastic walking spring toy, stretch it as you say words. **Note:** Remember, some phonemes are not *continuants* and cannot be stretched. Avoid adding "uh" to these sounds. For example, *ball* should be pronounced *baaaaaaaaalllllllllll*, with the initial, *noncontinuant* sound said briefly and the continuant sounds elongated (rather than *buuuuhhh—aaalll*). (See page 15 for more information.)

4. Contrast the stretched version of the word with the word as it is typically said. Repeat the two versions several times. If you are using a plastic walking spring toy, show it collapsed, then stretch it as you elongate the word. Engage in slow motion speech occasionally as children engage in other activities, such as cleaning up, moving outdoors, or selecting activities.

Modify or Extend

- Have children walk across the room as they slowly say their names. They begin their names on one side of the room and continue saying them as they move to the other side of the room. Do this in small groups, then let volunteers go individually.

- If you have enough toys for each child to hold one, invite children to stretch them as you all say words in slow motion. Make the toys available for later independent play.

Home Connection

Encourage children to share their names in slow motion with their families. If available, provide each child with a plastic walking spring toy to take home.

Slow Motion Speech (cont.)

Sample Words

Word	Slow Motion
ball	baaalll
cat	caaat
doll	dooolll
fan	fffaaannn
gum	guuummm
hand	hhhaaannnd
jam	jaaammm
key	keeey
lip	llliiip
man	mmmaaannn
nose	nnnooossse
run	rrruuunnn
sand	sssaaannnd
tree	trrreee
van	vvvaaannn
wind	wwwiiinnnd
zip	zzziiip

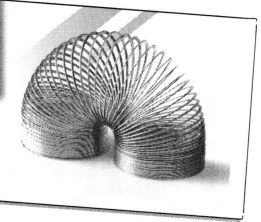

#50665—Purposeful Play for Early Childhood Phonological Awareness

Standards: Children discriminate among the sounds of spoken language. Children know that words are made up of sounds.

Beginning, Middle, or End?

Purpose

To segment words into phonemes; to identify a phoneme's location in a word

Overview

This activity is an extension of The Golden Touch activity. Here, the teacher asks children to identify whether a target sound is at the beginning, middle, or end of a word. To demonstrate the sound's location, children move a chip or other token into the first, middle, or last box drawn on a piece of paper to demonstrate the sound's location.

─Home Connection─

If children are interested, allow them to take home a phoneme boxes card and a chip so they can play Beginning, Middle, or End? with their families. Be sure the chips are large enough that they don't present a choking hazard.

Materials

card with three phoneme boxes (available on the Teacher Resource CD); chips, counters, or other tokens

Procedure

1. Share several words that begin with the same sound. Ask children what sound they hear at the beginning of the words, and if they can think of other words that start with that sound. Allow them to share their words, and provide gentle guidance and correction.

2. Share new words that have the same ending sounds, such as *duck*, *snack*, and *bike*. Ask children to say the words with you and emphasize the /k/ at the end of the word.

3. Share words that have the same middle sound, such as /ă/ in *hat*, *sad*, and *fan*. Emphasize the /ă/, and point out its middle position in the word.

4. Provide each child with a card with three boxes (see example) and a chip. Ask the children to listen for a particular sound and identify whether it is at the beginning, middle, or end of the word. As you say a word, children move a chip into the first box (on the left), the middle box, or the last box (on the right). Observe and assist children as they move their chips.

5. Share several sounds and words and ask children to place their chips in the beginning or end position in the boxes. (See examples in the table on the next page.)

Modify or Extend

- Begin by targeting continuant sounds because they will be easier to emphasize.

Beginning, Middle, or End? (cont.)

Sample Prompts

Teacher Says	Token Placement
Say /l/. Now say *tale*. Where is the /l/ sound in *tale*?	□ □ ⬤
Say /p/. Now say *pit*. Where is the /p/ sound in *pit*?	⬤ □ □
Say /n/. Now say *sun*. Where is the /n/ sound in *sun*?	□ □ ⬤
Say /ŏ/. Now say *hop*. Where is the /ŏ/ sound in *hop*?	□ ⬤ □
Say /s/. Now say *sit*. Where is the /s/ sound in *sit*?	⬤ □ □
Say /r/. Now say *run*. Where is the /r/ sound in *run*?	⬤ □ □
Say /g/. Now say *dog*. Where is the /g/ sound in *dog*?	□ □ ⬤
Say /ă/. Now say *hat*. Where is the /ă/ sound in *hat*?	□ ⬤ □

Standards: Children discriminate among the sounds of spoken language.
Children know that words are made up of sounds.

Elkonin Sound Boxes

Purpose

To segment words into phonemes

Overview

Elkonin Sound Boxes are simple drawings of boxes into which children move chips or other tokens for each sound they hear in a word. In this challenging activity, children view a picture of an object, say the name of the object, and then move chips into the boxes as they say each sound in the word. Teachers will likely wish to use this activity with very small groups or individuals so they can provide ample support and ensure success.

Home Connection

If children are successful, you may wish to send home the Elkonin Sound Box sheets and cards so they can share the activity with family members. As with all objects you give children, be careful to ensure that the chips are large enough that they don't present a choking hazard.

Materials

Elkonin Sound Box sheets (see examples on the next page; samples available on the Teacher Resource CD); chips, counters, or other tokens

Procedure

1. Present a picture of an object accompanied by a card with boxes equal to the number of phonemes in the word. For example, a picture of a fish would be accompanied by a card with three boxes, one for each of the three phonemes /f/—/ĭ/—/sh/ that constitute the word. A picture of a desk would be accompanied by a card with four boxes, one for each of the four phonemes /d/—/ĕ/—/s/—/k/. See the examples on the following page.

2. Give each child a set of chips and a card. Explain that they will move one chip into each sound box, starting with the box on the left, as they say each sound in the name of the object pictured. Demonstrate moving one chip for each sound in a word as you say it slowly. After you have moved all chips, say the word.

3. Ask children to move their chips as they repeat the word you just modeled. Provide feedback and support as needed.

4. Provide additional cards (available on the Teacher Resource CD) and support children as they identify the objects pictured. Slowly repeat the words, and move a chip for each sound they say.

Modify or Extend

- Consonant blends (such as /sk/ in *desk*) are generally difficult for young children to segment. Avoid using blends initially. Then provide plenty of support when you do.

Elkonin Sound Boxes (cont.)

Sample Elkonin Sound Boxes

© Shell Education   #50665—Purposeful Play for Early Childhood Phonological Awareness

Standards: Children discriminate among the sounds of spoken language. Children know that words are made up of sounds.

Break It!

Purpose

To segment words into phonemes

Overview

Children snap apart interlocking cubes as they segment words into sounds. This is a challenging activity that many young children may not be ready to undertake. Depending on the age and phonological abilities of children, you may wish to simply model it occasionally, for purposes of exposure.

Home Connection

Invite children to take home some of the plastic bags with cubes and objects to share with their families. If they wish, children may add other objects with the same number of sounds to the bag and bring the bag back to school to share.

Materials

one large bag that children cannot see through; many small plastic bags; interlocking cubes; a variety of small, familiar objects, each having a single-syllable name

Procedure

1. Select a variety of familiar objects, each of which has a single-syllable name. Place each object in its own sealed, clear plastic bag. Add enough connected interlocking cubes to each bag to correspond with the number of phonemes in the name of the object. For example, one bag might contain a key and two connected cubes for the two sounds in the word *key* (/k/—/ē/). Another bag might contain a leaf and three connected cubes for the three sounds in *leaf* (/l/—/ē/—/f/). (Additional suggestions are provided in the table on the next page.) Place all of the individual bags in a large grocery bag or box.

2. Have a child withdraw a small bag, open it, withdraw the object and the cubes, and hold them up for others to see. Ask the child to name the object.

3. Guide children to segment the name of the object into its constituent phonemes as the child holding the object breaks off one cube for each sound spoken.

4. Repeat the whole word and ask children to break apart the word as the volunteer holds up or reassembles the individual cubes, snapping them together as each sound is said. Play the game only as long as it holds children's interest.

Modify or Extend

-   Make the bags with objects and cubes available for children to handle and play with as they desire.

-   Consonant blends (such as /kl/ in *clock*) are more difficult for young children to segment. Avoid using words with blends initially. Then provide plenty of support when you do.

Break It! (cont.)

Sample Objects

Object	Word Segmented into Phonemes
ball	/b/—/ô/—/l/
book	/b/—/ŏŏ/—/k/
chip	/ch/—/ĭ/—/p/
comb	/c/—/ō/—/m/
dime	/d/—/ī/—/m/
nail	/n/—/ā/—/l/
pen	/p/—/ĕ/—/n/
ring	/r/—/ĭ/—/ng/
rock	/r/—/ŏ/—/k/
tape	/t/—/ā/—/p/
block	/b/—/l/—/ŏ/—/k/
brush	/b/—/r/—/ŭ/—/sh/
clock	/c/—/l/—/ŏ/—/k/
glue	/g/—/l/—/ōō/
sand	/s/—/ă/—/n/—/d/
stick	/s/—/t/—/ĭ/—/k/

Standards: Children discriminate among the sounds of spoken language. Children know that words are made up of sounds.

Simon Says

Purpose

To delete initial or final phonemes in words

Overview

Children play a game of Simon Says with the teacher. After telling them that Simon Says to touch their toes, hop, wave hello, and other actions, the teacher says that Simon wants them to say words without all their sounds. Children listen carefully to the words and then delete initial or final sounds, depending on the prompt.

Materials

Procedure

1. Teach children "Simon Says." Instruct children to listen carefully to directions and do only what you request when you preface it with "Simon says." If you say, "Stand up" without saying "Simon says," children should not stand up. Enjoy trying to catch children performing the actions when Simon doesn't say to do them. Allow children to play the role of Simon.

2. Ask children to say some words without all their sounds. Do not try to trick children with these requests—always use the "Simon says" prompt. Model some words for children and ask them to help you figure out what Simon wants you to say. For example, tell them that Simon wants you to say the word *part* without the /p/. What should you say? Help them determine that you should respond with the word *art*.

3. Enjoy helping children delete the sounds at the beginning of several words. On other occasions, have children delete final sounds in words. (See the tables for examples.)

Modify or Extend

- To increase the challenge for older children, use words containing blends and have children delete part of the blend. For example, ask them to say *stand* without the /t/, *black* without the /l/, *snack* without the /n/, and *drive* without the /r/.

Home Connection

Encourage families to play the traditional version of Simon Says.

Simon Says (cont.)

Sample Words for Initial Sound Deletion

Prompt: "Simon says..."	Response
Say *part*. Now say *part* without the /p/.	*art*
Say *pin*. Now say *pin* without the /p/.	*in*
Say *meat*. Now say *meat* without the /m/.	*eat*
Say *cup*. Now say *cup* without the /k/.	*up*
Say *cape*. Now say *cape* without the /k/.	*ape*
Say *rat*. Now say *rat* without the /r/.	*at*
Say *bone*. Now say *bone* without the /b/.	*own*
Say *hair*. Now say *hair* without the /h/.	*air*
Say *nice*. Now say *nice* without the /n/.	*ice*

Sample Words for Final Sound Deletion

Prompt: "Simon says..."	Response
Say *plate*. Now say *plate* without the /t/.	*play*
Say *date*. Now say *date* without the /t/.	*day*
Say *bead*. Now say *bead* without the /d/.	*bee*
Say *seed*. Now say *seed* without the /d/.	*see*
Say *drive*. Now say *drive* without the /v/.	*dry*
Say *heat*. Now say *heat* without the /t/.	*he*
Say *moat*. Now say *moat* without the /t/.	*mow*
Say *lake*. Now say *lake* without the /k/.	*lay*
Say *bake*. Now say *bake* without the /k/.	*bay*
Say *rope*. Now say *rope* without the /p/.	*row*
Say *cart*. Now say *cart* without the /t/.	*car*

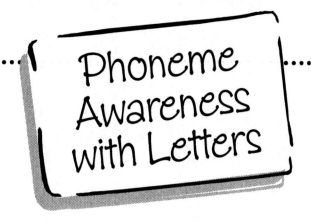

Phoneme Awareness with Letters

As children develop familiarity with the alphabet, letters may be included in phonological awareness activities. Research suggests that including letters in phonological awareness instruction supports both phonological development as well as letter knowledge.

Activity		Primary Task				
		identify	match	blend	segment	substitute
Initial Sounds	Post That Letter!	x	x			
	Sound Sort	x	x			
	Make a Change		x			x
	Willoughby Wallaby with Letters		x			x
	"A" Was Once an Apple Pie		x			x
	Draw a Card		x			x
Final Sounds	Add a Sound		x	x		
All Sounds	Make a Word		x		x	

Standards: Children know and can discriminate among sounds in words. Children use basic elements of phonetic word analysis.

Post That Letter!

Purpose

To identify initial phonemes in words; to match phonemes to letters

Overview

Children receive sticky notes on which a letter is written. The teacher names objects in the environment and children with the letter that represents the initial sound in the object's name affix the sticky note to the object.

Materials

sticky note paper; markers or crayons

Procedure

1. Select three or four letters children know and write each letter on several sticky papers. Give each child at least three copies of the same letter.

2. Ask children to show one another the sticky notes they were given and to tell one another the sound that is represented by their letter. Ask them to find someone else with the same letter. Share with the entire group the letters you have distributed and encourage each child to say each of the sounds.

3. Name an object in the environment. If a child has a letter that represents the initial sound in the object, he or she sticks it to the object. Because several children have the same letter, each object will have several sticky notes affixed to it.

4. Have children continue to select objects in the classroom that are appropriate matches for the letters you have distributed. Leave the sticky notes posted on the objects for the remainder of the day, or even for several days, and review the activity.

Modify or Extend

- Instead of giving each child three sticky notes of the same letter, give each child two or three different letters.

Home Connection

Make sticky notes and writing instruments available. Invite children to choose one of the letters you used in the activity, record it on several sticky notes, and take these home to affix to items in their home that begin with the corresponding sound. Encourage them to tell you about their findings the next day.

Post That Letter! *(cont.)*

Sample Objects

Letter	Object	Letter	Object
b	beanbag, board, basket	p	piano, pointer, pen
c	cabinet, calendar, clock	r	ribbon, rug, rope
d	desk, door, doll	s	seat, screen, sand
f	fishbowl, flag, floor	t	table, teacher, tray
j	jacket, jump rope, jacks	w	wall, window, wood
l	library, lost-and-found	y	yarn, yellow, yo-yo

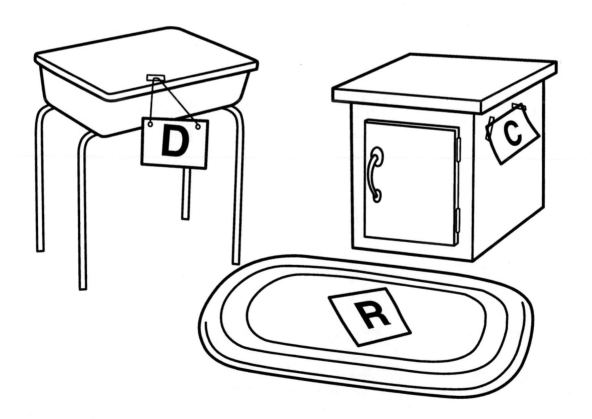

Sound Sort

Purpose

To identify initial phonemes in words; to match phonemes to letters

Overview

The teacher helps children explore and name familiar objects. Then they sort the objects into two piles based upon the object's initial phoneme, placing each object next to the appropriate letter card.

Materials

a variety of familiar objects, carefully selected based upon the initial phoneme; selected letter cards (available on the Teacher Resource CD)

Procedure

1. Gather objects that begin with either of two sounds you have targeted (based on children's familiarity with the letters and corresponding sounds). For example, if you have targeted /d/ and /k/, you might select a doll, a dollar, a dime, a kitten (toy), a kite, a key, and a ketchup bottle. Ask children to name the objects. Let them handle the objects and talk about them.

2. Show children the two letter cards and remind them of the sound each letter represents. Place the two letters apart from each other.

3. Have a child select an object. Ask him or her to name the object, identify the initial sound, and determine which letter represents that sound by placing the object next to that letter card.

4. Repeat the process with the other objects. After all objects have been placed next to the appropriate letter, draw children's attention to one group. Together, name all of the objects and ask if the objects sound alike at the beginning. Then, name the objects in the other group and point out the common initial sound.

Modify or Extend

- Make the letters available and invite children to find objects in the environment for later exploration.

- Have the children sort by final sounds. For the target sounds /d/ and /k/, for example, you might have the following picture cards or objects available: seed, hand, sled, bed, food, bike, piggy bank, rake, sock, and book. Assist children in identifying the objects as or before they sort them.

- Invite children to find objects in the environment that begin or end with the target sounds.

─ Home Connection ─

Invite families to share objects or pictures of objects from magazines or newspapers that begin with a letter you target. Display them on a board or table for children to handle and talk about. Prominently display the letter.

Sound Sort (cont.)

#50665—Purposeful Play for Early Childhood Phonological Awareness

Standards: Children know and can discriminate among sounds in words.
Children use basic elements of phonetic word analysis.

Make a Change

Purpose

To match phonemes to letters; to substitute initial phonemes in words

Overview

Use this activity once children have shown an interest in printed words and have some knowledge of sound-symbol correspondences. The teacher presents a word from a word family, such as *hat* from the *-at* family. Children change the word by placing a new letter over the initial letter in the original word. Then they say the new word.

Materials

large 4" x 6" sticky notes with letters written on them; word cards or a whiteboard and marker

Procedure

1. Write a word on a large card or whiteboard. Make sure the word is written large enough so the initial letter can be covered with a new letter that is easily seen by everyone in the group.

2. Pronounce the word with children. Ask them to repeat the word. Then, ask them to say only the first sound in the word.

3. Display several sticky notes, each of which has a single letter written on it. Invite a child to select one of the sticky notes. Encourage all children to say the sound the letter represents. Respond enthusiastically to their accurate responses or gently remind them of the sound if they need support.

4. Ask the child to place the sticky note over the initial letter in the word. Have children say the new word. Provide support as needed.

5. Remove the sticky note and have children tell you the original word. Place and remove the sticky note several times, and have children say each word as you show the initial letter.

6. Invite another child to select a different sticky note to place over the initial letter in the word. Continue with other sticky notes for a few minutes or as long as it holds children's attention.

Modify or Extend

- Extend this activity with other word families. See the table on the next page for suggestions.

Home Connection

Make a large word card and several sticky notes with appropriate letters available for children to share with family members.

Make a Change (cont.)

Sample Word Families

Original Word	Word Family	Letters for Other Words			
pan	-an	c (can)		f (fan)	
		m (man)		r (ran)	
		t (tan)		v (van)	
lap	-ap	c (cap)		g (gap)	
		m (map)		r (rap)	
		s (sap)		t (tap)	
tell	-ell	b (bell)		f (fell)	
		s (sell)		w (well)	
		y (yell)			
hen	-en	d (den)		m (men)	
		p (pen)		t (ten)	
big	-ig	d (dig)		f (fig)	
		r (rig)		w (wig)	
lip	-ip	d (dip)		h (hip)	
		s (sip)		t (tip)	
sit	-it	b (bit)		f (fit)	
		h (hit)		l (lit)	
		p (pit)		w (wit)	
dog	-og	f (fog)		h (hog)	
		j (jog)		l (log)	
hop	-op	m (mop)		p (pop)	
		t (top)			
dug	-ug	b (bug)		h (hug)	
		j (jug)		r (rug)	
		t (tug)			
run	-un	b (bun)		f (fun)	
		s (sun)			

Standards: Children know and can discriminate among sounds in words. Children use basic elements of phonetic word analysis.

Willoughby Wallaby with Letters

Purpose

To match phonemes to letters; to substitute initial phonemes in names

Overview

In an earlier activity the teacher substituted different initial sounds in the words of this song. Now the teacher shows the corresponding letter by using name cards and holding a letter card over the initial letter of a child's name. This connects the letter changes to the sound changes.

┌Home Connection ┐

Invite children to take home their name cards and two or three letters and to share the song with family members. In addition, provide in writing, at individuals' requests, any other names children would like to take home. Some children may say *Mommy*, *Grandma*, *Opa*, or the proper names of family members.

Materials

one card for each child with his or her name; letter cards from the Teacher Resource CD

Procedure

1. Remind children of the song "Willoughby Wallaby Woo." Use children's names and substitute the initial sound in their names with the /w/ sound.

2. Write children's names on individual strips of card stock. Hold up a name and ask children to say it. Show children a letter card and together remind them the sound the letter represents. For example, remind children that *"w"* generally represents the /w/ sound.

3. Place the "W" letter card over the initial letter on the name card. If you are showing Tommy's name, place a "W" over the "T" in his name. Together say Tommy's name with the substituted sound: *Tommy* becomes *Wommy*.

4. Sing the song, using children's name cards and holding the "W" over the initial letter at the appropriate point in the song. Use other letter cards, as appropriate. **Note:** Some names begin with a vowel sound. In these cases, add the selected phoneme to the beginning of the name. For example, *Emily* becomes *Wemily* and *Alice* becomes *Walice*.

Modify or Extend

- Be sure that the letters are ones with which children have experience. You may wish to have several available and let children select the card they would like to use for the next rendition of the song.

Willoughby Wallaby with Letters (cont.)

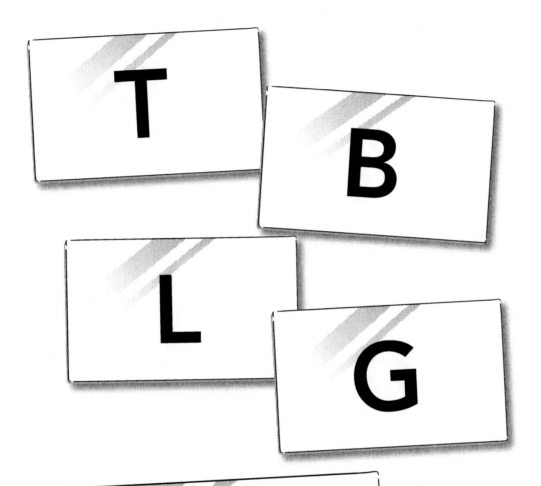

"Willoughby Wallaby Woo"

Willoughby Wallaby Woo,

An elephant sat on you.

Willoughby Wallaby Wee,

An elephant sat on me.

#50665—Purposeful Play for Early Childhood Phonological Awareness

Standards: Children know and can discriminate among sounds in words. Children use basic elements of phonetic word analysis.

"A" Was Once an Apple Pie

Purpose

To substitute initial phonemes in words; to match phonemes to letters

Overview

After reading this alphabet book in which the author uses nonsensical rhymes, the teacher invites children to generate new words by substituting phonemes and then create their own alphabet book.

Materials

"A" Was Once an Apple Pie by Edward Lear (2005); large and small sheets of paper; markers or crayons; glue; box filled with a variety of picture cards or objects (optional); magazines or other sources of pictures (optional) (pictures are available on the Teacher Resource CD)

Procedure

1. Read aloud "A" Was Once an Apple Pie and point out the silly language play on each page. Have children join in the language play by generating their own words to add to the story.

2. Construct a group book for a few letters of the alphabet. Have children choose a letter, identify its sound, and name an object that begins with the sound.

3. Model using the author's pattern to create a page for your book. An example for the letters "d" and "t" are shown on the next page.

4. Record children's ideas on large pieces of paper, one letter per page, and compile the papers into a book. Before binding the book, allow children to illustrate the pages, if they would like to do so. Or, have children find pictures of objects in magazines to cut out and glue them to the pages of the book.

Modify or Extend

- To assist children in finding objects that can represent different letters of the alphabet. Prepare a box of picture cards or objects—including at least one object for each letter of the alphabet—and allow children to look through the box for ideas. ("What starts with /d/? Oh! I see a toy dog!") **Note:** "X" at the beginning of words usually represents the /z/ sound. Children are taught that the letter "x" represents /ks/. Teachers should be thoughtful about how to use this letter in this activity and select an object that matches their letter sound instruction.

Home Connection

Use smaller sheets of paper for your group book and make a photocopy for each child. Children may ask family members to read their book.

"A" Was Once an Apple Pie (cont.)

Sample Page

Letter	Sample Page
d	"D" was once a little dog Doggy Zoggy Poggy Coggy Cutey Doggy Little dog
t	"T" was once a tasty treat Treaty Featy Peaty Weaty Tiny treat Tasty treat

Draw a Card

Purpose

To match phonemes to letters; to substitute initial phonemes in words

Overview

In this activity, children draw letters from a container to replace the initial letters and sounds in the phrase "Ding! Ding! Dong!" after learning the song "Are You Sleeping?"

Materials

alphabet letter cards (capital letters, consonants only, available on the Teacher Resource CD); whiteboard and marker; bells for several or all children (*optional*); paper bags (*optional*)

Procedure

1. Teach or review the song, "Are You Sleeping?" (available on the Teacher Resource CD). Provide children with bells to ring during the final two lines if you wish.

2. Repeat the words "Ding! Ding! Dong!" Ask children what they notice about these three words. (They all begin with the same sound: /d/.) Ask children if they know what letter is used to write the /d/ sound.

3. Write "Ding! Ding! Dong!" on the board. Point out that the letter "D" is at the beginning of each word.

4. Show children a container of letter cards. Ask a child to draw a card, identify the letter, and discuss the sound it represents. Erase the "D" from the phrase on the whiteboard and replace it with the new consonant. Sing the song with the new words.

5. Children continue to draw cards, replacing the initial letters in the words, and singing the newly created phrases.

Modify or Extend

- Allow children to select two or three letters from the container and replace each "D" with a different letter. If they select the two letters "R" and "P," for example, they would sing "Ring! Ring! Pong!" If they select "R," "S," and "P," they would sing "Ring! Sing! Pong!"

- Add consonant blends to the container.

Home Connection

Post the lyrics to the song in a newsletter, or on a class website. Give children a paper bag that contains several letter cards. Encourage them to share the activity with their families and to think of new versions of "Ding! Ding! Dong!" to share with the class.

Draw a Card (cont.)

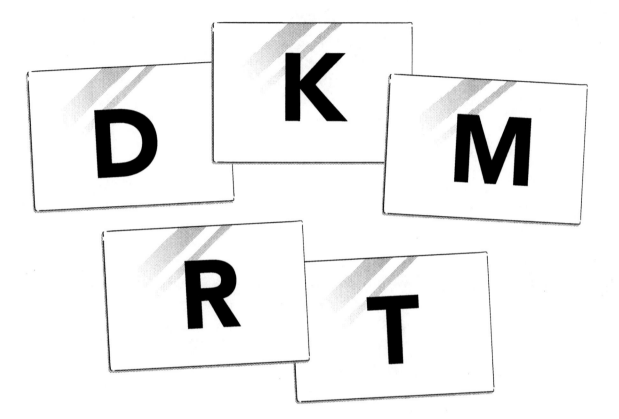

"Are You Sleeping?"

Are you sleeping?

Are you sleeping?

Brother John,

Brother John.

Morning bells are ringing,

Morning bells are ringing.

Ding! Ding! Dong!

Ding! Ding! Dong!

#50665—Purposeful Play for Early Childhood Phonological Awareness

Standards: Children know and can discriminate among sounds in words. Children use basic elements of phonetic word analysis.

Add a Sound

Purpose

To add phonemes to words (blending); to match phonemes to letters; to blend phonemes

Overview

The teacher reads a story in which the /ō/ sound has been added to the end of several words. The teacher discusses the sound play, and presents the letter "O." Children use a letter card to add the /ō/ sound to objects in the room and to objects in drawings.

Materials

The Fox Went Out on a Chilly Night by Peter Spier (1994); several large cards on which the letter "O" is written; one smaller letter card with the letter "O" for each member of the class (*optional*); materials for drawing (*optional*); string, ribbon, or yarn (*optional*)

Procedure

1. Read *The Fox Went Out on a Chilly Night*. Point out how the sound /ō/ is added to many words: *town-o, tail-o, down-o, bones-o*. Reread the story and have children repeat the words with the /ō/ addition.

2. Have children indicate if they know the letter that is used to make the /ō/ sound at the end of those words. Make an "O" with your fingers, with your arms, and with your mouth. Have children share other ways to make the shape of the letter "O." Then have children form a large "O" on the floor by sitting in a circle.

3. Show large cards with the letter "O" and give cards to several children. Sing or chant the following while children pass the cards clockwise: "Pass the cards, Pass the cards, Pass the cards, 'Til the fox runs home!"

4. Have children who are holding a card when the word *home* is sung stand up and find something to touch. Instruct them to touch their "O" card to the objects, and then have all children say the name of the object, adding the /ō/ sound to the end (for example, *floor-o, chair-o, cubby-o*). Ask children to return to their places in the circle and begin the chanting and passing of the cards again.

Modify or Extend

- Have children draw pictures of anything they wish. Attach a string, ribbon, or yarn to the corner of their papers. On the free end of the string, attach a small piece of paper with the letter "O" printed on it. Have children touch the letter to the objects in their pictures and say the names with the added /ō/ sound.

┌Home Connection┐

Provide all children with an "O" letter card to take home. Invite them to tell you what they will touch and to bring objects to school with them, if they wish, to show you how they can name the object with the added sound.

Add a Sound (cont.)

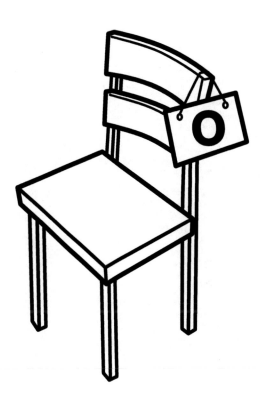

Standards: Children discriminate among the sounds of spoken language.
Children know that words are made up of sounds.
Children use basic elements of phonetic word analysis.

Make a Word

Purpose

To segment words into phonemes; to match phonemes with letters

Overview

This activity is appropriate for children who know some sound-symbol correspondences and who have shown some ability to segment short words into their constituent phonemes. Children repeat a word shared by the teacher, segment the word, and select from a small number of letter cards those necessary to create the word. Ample scaffolding should be provided.

─Home Connection─

Provide a small set of letters for children to take home. Encourage them to share some of the words they can construct with the letters. Be sure that you have practiced this with children sufficiently.

Materials

selected letter cards, one set for each child; list of words that can be created from the letters provided for the teacher's reference (see the table for suggestions)

Procedure

1. Construct a small set of selected letter cards for each child, or print them from the Teacher Resource CD. Review the sound each letter represents. Have each child lay his or her letter cards in a line so they can be seen.

2. Say, "Listen to this word: *cat*." Ask children to repeat it. Assist children in segmenting the word. Say the word again slowly. Ask children to identify the first sound in the word. Ask them which letter represents that sound, and have them move that letter to start building the word.

3. Say the word again. Assist children in identifying the next sound in the word. Have them move the appropriate letter into position to continue building the word. Repeat for the remaining sound in the word. Say each sound represented by the letters and then say the whole word.

4. Change one letter to make a new word. Say this new word. For example, change the "*c*" in *cat* to an "*r*", and say, "rat." Break the word into phonemes: /r/—/ă/—/t/.

5. Continue making new words with the set of letter cards, using the suggestions in the table on the next page as a guide.

Modify or Extend

- On other occasions, provide different sets of letters and try building other words, such as those displayed in the table on the next page.

Make a Word (cont.)

Sample Letter Sets and Words

Letter Cards	Possible Words
c, r, l, p, t, a	cat, rat, pat, tap, cap, trap, clap, lap
h, m, n, p, s, t, e	men, hen, hem, ten, nest, step, pest
f, h, m, n, s, t, i	it, hit, tin, fin, sit, him, mist
f, g, p, r, s, t, o	frog, fog, got, rot, top, pot, stop, tops, pots
b, f, n, t, s, u	sun, bun, fun, nut, nuts, stun

#50665—Purposeful Play for Early Childhood Phonological Awareness

References Cited

Adams, M. J. 1990. *Beginning to read: Thinking and learning about print*. Cambridge, MA: MIT.

Anthony, J. L., C. J. Lonigan, K. Driscoll, B. M. Phillips, and S. R. Burgess. 2003. Preschool phonological sensitivity: A quasi-parallel progression of word structure units and cognitive operations. *Reading Research Quarterly*, no. 38: 470–487.

Burgess, S. R. 2006. The development of phonological sensitivity. In D. K. Dickinson and S. B. Neuman (Eds.) *Handbook of early literacy research* (Vol. 2, pp. 90–100). New York: Guilford.

Ehri, L. C., S. R. Nunes, D. M. Willows, B. V. Schuster, Z. Yaghoub-Zadeh, and T. Shanahan. 2001. Phonemic awareness instruction helps students learn to read: Evidence from the National Reading Panel's meta-analysis. *Reading Research Quarterly*, 36, 250–287.

Ehri, L. C., and T. Roberts. 2006. The roots of learning to read and write: Acquisition of letters and phonemic awareness. In D. K. Dickinson and S. B. Neuman (Eds.) *Handbook of early literacy research* (Vol. 2, pp. 113–131). New York: Guilford.

Flanigan, K. 2007. A concept of word in text: A pivotal event in early reading acquisition. *Journal of Literacy Research*, 39, 37–70.

Gillon, Gail. 2004. *Phonological awareness: From research to practice*. New York: Guilford Press.

Joshi, R. M., and P. G. Aaron (Eds.). 2006. *Handbook of orthography and literacy*. Mahwah, NJ: Lawrence Erlbaum.

Liberman, I., D. Shankweiler, F. Fischer, and B. Carter. 1974. Explicit syllable and phoneme segmentation in the young child. *Journal of Experimental Child Psychology*, 18, 201–212.

Lonigan, C. J. 2006. Conceptualizing phonological processing skills in prereaders. In D. K. Dickinson and S. B. Neuman (Eds.) *Handbook of early literacy research* (Vol. 2, pp. 77–89). New York: Guilford.

Mann, V. A. and J. G. Foy. 2003. Phonological awareness, speech development, and letter knowledge in preschool students. *Annals of Dyslexia*, 53, 149–173.

Moats, L. C. 2005–06. How spelling supports reading: And why it is more regular and predictable than you may think. *American Educator*. 29(4),12–22, 42-43.

———. 2000. *Speech to print: Language essentials for teachers*. Baltimore: Brookes.

Moats, L., and C. Tolman. 2008. The development of phonological skills. In *Reading Rockets*. Washington, D. C.: U.S. Department of Education: Reading Rockets. (www.readingrockets.org/articles/28759)

National Early Literacy Panel. 2008. *Developing early literacy: Report of the National Early Literacy Panel*. Washington, DC: National Institute for Literacy.

National Reading Panel. 2000. *Teaching students to read: An evidence-based assessment of the scientific research literature on reading and its implications for reading instruction*. Washington, DC: National Institute of Child Health and Human Development.

Phillips. B. M., J. Clancy-Menchetti, and C. J. Lonigan. 2008. Successful phonological awareness instruction with preschool students. *Topics in Early Childhood Special Education*, 28, 3–17.

References Cited *(cont.)*

Phillips, B. M., and J. K. Torgesen. 2006. Phonemic awareness and reading: Beyond the growth of initial reading accuracy. In D. K. Dickinson & S. B. Neuman (Eds.), *Handbook of early literacy research* (Vol. 2, pp. 101–112). New York: Guilford.

Sainz, J. S. 2006. Literacy acquisition in Spanish. In R. M. Joshi and P. G. Aaron (Eds.), *Handbook of orthography and literacy* (pp. 151–170). Mahwah, NJ: Lawrence Erlbaum.

Shaywitz, S. 2003. *Overcoming dyslexia*. New York: Knopf

Smith, S. B., Simmons, D. C., and Kame'enui, E. J. 1998. Phonological awareness: Instructional and curricular basics and implications. In D. C. Simmons and E. J. Kame'enui (Eds.), *What reading research tells us about children with diverse learning needs: Bases and basics* (pp. 129–140). Mahwah, NJ: Lawrence Erlbaum.

Valtin, R. 1984. Awareness of features and functions of language. In J. Downing and R. Valtin (Eds.), *Phonological awareness in reading: The evolution of current perspectives* (pp. 1–30). New York: Springer-Verlag.

Yopp, H. K. 1992. Developing phonemic awareness in young students. *The Reading Teacher*, 45, 696–703.

———. 1999. Phonemic awareness: Frequently asked questions. *The California Reader*, 32(4), 21–27.

———. 1995. Read-aloud books for developing phonemic awareness: An annotated bibliography. *The Reading Teacher*, 48, 538–542.

———. 1988. The validity and reliability of phonemic awareness tests. *Reading Research Quarterly*, 23, 159–177

Yopp, H. K., and L. Stapleton. 2008. Conciencia fonémica en español (Phonemic awareness in Spanish). *The Reading Teacher*. 61, 374–382.

Yopp, H. K., and R. H. Yopp. 2002. *Oo-pples and boo-noo-noos: Songs and activities for phonemic awareness*, 2nd ed. Orlando: Harcourt School Publishers.

———. 2009. Phonological awareness is child's play! *Young Students*. 64(1), 12-21. [Extended version in NAEYC's online *Beyond the Journal*]

———. 2000. Supporting phonemic awareness development in the classroom. *The Reading Teacher*, 54, 130–143.

Bibliography of Literature: Books

Ada, A. F. and F. I. Campoy. *¡Pío Peep! Rimas tradicionales en Español*. Edición especial. New York: HarperCollins, 2003.

Ahlberg, Janet and Allan Ahlberg. *Each Peach Pear Plum*. New York: Puffin Books, 1986.

Bynum, Janie. *Altoona Baboona*. San Diego, CA: Sandpiper, 2002.

Craft, Charlotte. *King Midas and the Golden Touch*. New York: HarperCollins, 1999.

Delgado, Henry. *Destrabalenguerias para trabalngueros*. Bogotá, Columbia: Circulo de Lectores, Intermedio, 2008.

Dewdney, Anna. *Llama Llama Red Pajama*. New York: Viking Juvenile, 2005.

Florian, Douglas. *Laugh-eteria*. Orlando, FL: Harcourt Brace & Co., 2008.

Isecke, Harriet. *The Sojourner Truth Story: Expanding and Preserving the Union*. Huntington Beach, CA: Teacher Created Materials, 2009.

Lear, Edward. *"A" Was Once an Apple Pie*. London: Orchard Books, 2005.

Longo, Alejandra. *Aserrin Aserran: Las canciones de la abuela: Las Canciones De La Abuela*. Translation. New York: Scholastic en Espanol, 2004.

Mosel, Arlene. *Tikki Tikki Tembo*. New York: Henry Holt & Co., 2007.

Moss, Jeff. Ankylosaurus. *Bone Poems*. New York: Workman Publishing Company, 1997.

Most, Bernard. *Cock-a-Doodle Moo!* Orlando, FL: Harcourt Brace & Co., 1996.

Rasinski, Timothy and Lorraine Griffith. *Building Fluency Through Practice and Performance, Grade 2*. Huntington Beach, CA: Shell Education, 2008.

Robleda, Margarita. *Numeros Tragaldabas*. Mexico: Planeta, 2003.

Rosen, Michael. *We're Going on a Bear Hunt*. New York: Little Simon, 1997.

Seidler, Ann and Jan Slepian. *The Hungry Thing*. New York: Scholastic, 2001.

————. *The Hungry Thing Goes to a Restaurant*. New York: Scholastic, 1993.

Seuss, Dr. *Hay Un Molillo En Mi Bolsillo!* Translation. New York: Lectorum Publications, 2007.

Seuss, Dr. *There's a Wocket in My Pocket!* Book club edit. New York: Random House Books for Young Readers, 1974.

Showers, Paul. *The Listening Walk*. New York: HarperCollins, 1993.

Silverstein, Shel. Pinocchio. In *Falling Up*. 2nd ed. New York: HarperCollins, 1996.

The Three Billy Goats Gruff (any version).

Waber, Bernard. *Bearsie Bear and the Surprise Sleepover Party*. New York: Houghton Mifflin Harcourt, 2002.

Yolen, Jane. *Off We Go!* New York: Little, Brown Books for Young Readers, 2000.

Bibliography of Literature: Chants, Rhymes, and Songs

Christelow, Eileen. *Five Little Monkeys Jumping on the Bed*. New York: Clarion Books, 1989.

C.R.S. Players, The. Heads, Shoulders, Knees, and Toes. CRS Records, 2007.

Cummings, Pat. *My Aunt Came Back*. New York: HarperFestival, 1998.

Degen, Bruce. *Jamberry*. New York: Scholastic, 1990.

Ives, Penny. *Five Little Ducks*. Auburn, ME: Child's Play International, Ltd. 2002.

Langstaff, John. *Oh, A-Hunting We Will Go*. Fullerton, CA: Aladdin, 1991.

Lee, Dennis. *Willoughby Wallaby Woo*. Toronto, Ontario: Key Porter Books, 1983.

Miller, Mitchell. *One Misty, Moisty Morning: Rhymes from Mother Goose*. 1st ed. New York: Farrar Straus & Giroux (J), 1971.

Raffi. Down By the Bay, et al. *The Singable Songs Collection*. Rounder/Umgd, 1996.

Rideout, Bonnie. Have You Ever Seen A Lassie? *Gi'me Elbow Room*. Shady Side, MD: Maggie's Music, 1998.

Schiller, Pam and Thomas Moore. *Do You Know the Muffin Man?: Literacy Activities Using Favorite Rhymes and Songs*. Silver Spring, MD: Gryphon House, 2004.

Sherman, Richard M. and Robert B. Sherman. It's a Small World song lyrics—Words for the It's a Small World ride at Disneyland, Walt Disney World Magic Kingdom, Tokyo Disneyland, 1965.

Spier, Peter. *London Bridge Is Falling Down (The Mother Goose Library)*. New York: Doubleday Books for Young Readers, 1985.

———. *The Fox Went Out on a Chilly Night*. New York: Dell Dragonfly, 1994.

———. *To Market! To Market!* New York: Yearling, 1992.

Traditional, and Adapted by Lorraine Bayes. Clap, Clap, Clap Your Hands. Bloomfield Hills, MI: Songs for Teaching® Using Music to Promote Learning, 2002.

Wells, Rosemary. *The Bear Went Over The Mountain*. New York: Scholastic Press, 1998.

Zelinsky, Paul O. *The Wheels on the Bus*. New York: Dutton Juvenile, 2000.

Contents of Teacher Resource CD

Family Involvement	
Letter to Families	letterhome.pdf
The Hungry Thing Letter 1	hungrything1.pdf
The Hungry Thing Letter 2	hungrything2.pdf
Suggested Rhymes	rhymes.pdf
Picture Cards	
Letters	lettercards.pdf
Single Syllable Words	wordcards1.pdf
Multisyllabic (noncompound) Words	wordcards2.pdf
Compound Words	wordcards3.pdf
Food Items	foodcards.pdf
Animals	animalcards.pdf
Templates	
Blank Sound Bingo Card	bingo.pdf bingo.doc
Phoneme Boxes	boxes.pdf
Elkonin Boxes	Elkonin.pdf
Puppets	puppets.pdf
Lyrics	
"Five Little Monkeys Jumping on the Bed"	five_little_monkeys.pdf
"The Bear Went Over the Mountain"	bear_went_over_the_mountain.pdf
"The Wheels on the Bus"	wheels_on_the_bus.pdf

Contents of Teacher Resource CD

"Five Little Ducks"	five_little_ducks.pdf
"London Bridge is Falling Down"	london_bridge.pdf
"Mr. Sun"	mr_sun.pdf
"Did You Ever See a Lassie?"	lassie.pdf
"Clap, Clap, Clap Your Hands"	clap.pdf
"Hickory Dickory Dock"	hickory_dickory.pdf
"Down By the Bay"	down_by_the_bay.pdf
"My Aunt Came Back"	my_aunt.pdf
"The Corner Grocery Store"	grocery_store.pdf
"A-Hunting We Will Go"	a_hunting.pdf
"The Muffin Man"	muffin_man.pdf
"Willougby Wallaby Woo"	willoughby_wallaby.pdf
"Pop! Goes the Weasel"	pop.pdf
"The Farmer in the Dell"	farmer_in_the_dell.pdf
"Head, Shoulders, Knees, and Toes"	head_shoulders.pdf
"Are You Sleeping?"	are_you_sleeping.pdf
"The Ants Go Marching"	ants.pdf
Spanish Resources	
Traditional Spanish Songs and Poems	spanishsongs.pdf
Spanish Literature	spliterature.pdf

192

#50665—Purposeful Play for Early Childhood Phonological Awareness   © Shell Education